SALISBURY CITY HALL

THROUGH THE LOOKING GLASS

Other titles by James McCarraher:

The Adventures of the Wandelsnop (1996)
The History of the City Hall, Salisbury (1998)
The Sailor Story (2004)
The Sailor Story (Reprint) (2005)
An Office Haunting (2006)
Kajanus: The Biography* (2006)
Angel Air Is Ten (2007)
An Office Haunting (5th Anniversary) (2011)
A Brooklands Ghost (2011)
The Sailor Scrapbook (2011)
A Book of Nonsense Verse** (2011)
The Sailor Scrapbook - Kindle version (2012)
An Office Haunting (5th Anniversary) – Kindle version (2012)
A Brooklands Ghost - Kindle version (2012)
A Book of Nonsense Verse** - Kindle version (2012)
101 Songs To Discover From The Seventies (2012)
101 Songs To Discover From The Seventies – Kindle version (2012)

*Co-authored with Georg Kajanus

**Project Editor.

SALISBURY CITY HALL

THROUGH

THE

LOOKING GLASS

By James McCarraher

Foreword by City Hall Manager

Phill Smith

Copyright © 2013 James McCarraher.

ISBN: 978-1-291-31479-3

The Author asserts his right to be identified as the author of this work in accordance with Sections 77 to 78 of the Copyright, Designs and Patents Act 1988.
All rights reserved. No part of this book may be reproduced in any form or by any electronic or mechanical means, including information storage or retrieval systems, without permission in writing from the publisher, except by a reviewer who may quote brief passages.

A catalogue record for this book is available from the British Library.

CONTENTS

Forward	7
Introduction	11
Putting You in the Picture	17
Opening Day	23
The Programme	33
The War Years	43
The Post War Years	55
Oscar Deutsch Entertains Our Nation	67
A New Hall for Salisbury	81
The Sixties Pop Dances	99
The Seventies	109
Wrestling in the Seventies	117
Amateur in Name Only	131
White Elephant?	141
Re-make Re-Model	151
Phoenix	165
Into the 21st Century	183

Nova Pilbeam Filmography 197

SAOS Productions at the City Hall 199

Acknowledgements Credits and Thanks 204

Photographs 205

FOREWORD

'Think Live Entertainment, Think City Hall Salisbury'

Our strap line is '*Think Live Entertainment, Think City Hall Salisbury*' which reflects why we have continued to thrive in an age where it is all too easy to stay indoors and be entertained. It's the live experience that counts!

Whether that is a great band, a comedian making us laugh or one of the many talented local groups that regularly perform on the City Hall stage, there really is nothing like seeing a live performance in a friendly and welcoming atmosphere.

For the last fifty years, City Hall has been right at the centre of the community, not just in Salisbury but reaching right across Wiltshire and the wider region. We are reminded that City Hall as we know it today exists because of the selfless sacrifice of those citizens who gave their lives in two world wars, and the generosity of those who contributed to the memorial fund to honour those citizens of Salisbury that had paid such a high cost. The contributors to that fund, combined with financial support from the old Salisbury City Council, meant that conversion from a cinema to a live entertainment venue was possible, and our history is reflected in the naming of our function room (Alamein Suite) and in the annual remembrance festival which the Royal British Legion continue to hold in City Hall every year.

At intervals over the years, the future of City Hall has been reviewed, and we have always been struck by the genuine affection that City Hall is held in by members of the public and the local community. I'm reminded of the gentleman who wrote to the Salisbury Journal, and said that although he never used City Hall, he did not begrudge a single penny of his council tax being spent on the service as it obviously gave so much pleasure to those who did. His comment and the thanks of other users give our team a real sense of job satisfaction as have the high ratings awarded by external assessment and the consistent positive customer response in monthly surveys.

Sales have continued to be strong, despite the difficult economic times and none of this would be possible without the hard work of the truly talented and committed teams that have worked at

City Hall across the years, alongside the support, enthusiasm and commitment that council members have provided and which has secured the venue for future generations.

We also enjoy being a part of the Salisbury business community and would like to take a moment to recognise all of the businesses, media and arts and cultural organisations that we have the pleasure of working with, you know who you are and we say thank you. City Hall is probably unique amongst venues as it has the privilege of also being home to the studios of the local radio station Spire FM, who celebrated their 20th anniversary in 2012. In the same year, the building reached its 75th anniversary.

Since opening on 30th January 1963, the City Hall can celebrate being the venue which has bought the following acts to Salisbury. From the world of music: Beverley Knight, Joan Armatrading, Morrissey, Joan Baez, N-Dubz, Hank Marvin, Bill Wyman and Brian May. From the world of comedy: Ken Dodd, the late Norman Wisdom, Billy Connolly to newer comedy superstars like Michael McIntyre, Peter Kay, Russell Brand, Russell Howard, Dara O'Brian, Sarah Millican, Jimmy Carr and John Bishop. Let us not forget the shows, which our audiences love and return to see year after year including 'That'll Be the Day', Moscow Ballet La Classique, and many 60s reunion tours such as The Solid Silver 60s Show.

The list is truly endless. There have been many marvellous performances from local performers including the Salisbury Amateur Operatic Society, now known as Musical Theatre Salisbury and Salisbury Dance Studios, the Salisbury Area Young Musicians and the Salisbury Symphony Orchestra.

Not all of you will be aware, but many students have crossed our front doors in order to take an exam and I think it is important to also pay tribute to those young people and the many others that over the years have endured examinations in these rooms. Not many people can say that they have taken an exam in the same room that The Beatles have performed!

Some of you may have memories of attending these events. Perhaps you were one of the young girls that stormed that stage when local boys Dave Dee, Dozy, Beaky, Mick and Tich performed, or you remember the golden years of all-in wrestling, or the regular roller discos. Perhaps you work or have worked as part of the team at City Hall?

In closing, I would like to offer my thanks and gratitude to Councillor Mrs Scott, who as Leader of Wiltshire Council decided in 2009, along with her colleagues, that City Hall should be transferred to the new Wiltshire Council. The venue continues to grow and develop and with the commitment shown by the Council, we look forward to another fifty glorious years.

I would also like to extend my personal thanks to the current City Hall team who continue to provide me with such valuable support and to the many who continue to buy tickets –

I wish you many more memorable nights at City Hall.

Phill Smith
Manager

INTRODUCTION

It was on the occasion of the building's 60th anniversary, I set about writing the history of the building as a cinema. The end result was a short book with a long title:

'Story Of The City Hall Part One – The Cinema Years 1937-1961.'

So why did I call, it 'Part One', and where are the other volumes?

Well, the idea at the time was to produce a series of three books. The second and third in the series were going to cover 1962-1980 and 1981-1998 respectively…but they never happened.

In 1999 I received a promotion from my day job and moved away from the area to Surrey. Fatherhood and other changes in my life re-organised priorities and the projects never got any further.

The release of the first volume in November 1998 was a huge success. Phill Smith (then and still) Manager of the City Hall and his kind and dedicated staff organised a book launch in the Alamein Suite on the same night that George Melly and Humphrey Lyttleton were in town (sadly, neither are no longer with us).

Our guests of honour were Olwyn Tanner (then Mayor) and Rosemary Squire, our local jazz legend. We also invited along staff both past and present including projectionist Ken Robson, his wife Beryl and Chief Usherette Muriel Eldridge. This was Muriel's first visit to the building since the cinema closed in 1961!

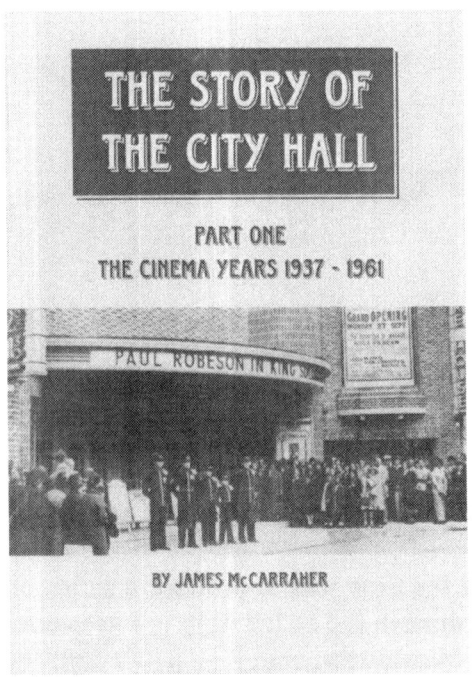

There were speeches, a cake cutting and a good time was had by all.

The Salisbury Journal loved the publication. Angela Turnbull had this to say:

"A treasure. You can positively feel the glamour of the City Hall cinema years. Not to be missed if you enjoy cinema history, social history or Salisbury history."

'Story Of The City Hall Part One – The Cinema Years 1937-1961' went on to sell six hundred copies in just six weeks and topped the Christmas best sellers list in Salisbury, outselling every other book in the City. Not only was this a matter of great personal pride, but it also made me realise just how loved and valued our City Hall was, and still is today.

So, back to Volumes Two and Three. In 2009, I relocated back from Surrey to the South Coast and during the move, discovered an enormous folder packed full of research and photographs from my time in Salisbury.

As I delved into the unpublished photographs, newspaper cuttings, letters and notes, I realised that I had hardly scratched the surface with the first book; there was so much more of the story to tell. Indeed much of the research from the cinema years had not been utilised for reasons known only to me at the time.

I therefore took the decision to re-visit the original book, which has now been re-written, considerably expanded and populated with new, unpublished photographs and interviews and crowned with a reprint of the original opening day programme! This makes up the first stage of this publication.

But the book does not stop there. The story moves onward to capture the City Hall years, through the glory days of the Sixties, the desperate Seventies, the renaissance in the Eighties and Nineties and into the 21st Century, thereby bringing the story right up to date for the very first time.

In 2012, the building reached its landmark 75th year of service, both as a cinema and an entertainment venue. And in 2013, the

City Hall hit its magic half century, celebrated once again with speeches and a cake cutting.

It has not been an easy task writing the later history of the building. With a cinema, there is continuity of use, making the story easier to tell. The City Hall was used for wrestling, ballet, amateur operatics, dinner dances, rock concerts and much more besides. It has been hard to balance all of these competing events, but I hope the end result is a reasonably coherent read. It has not been possible to cover every event and there will be many stories to tell besides those included in this book, but I hope you will agree that it provides a decent overview of a much loved building that has experienced some incredible high points and more than its fair share of lows as well.

The pictures in this book tell a story as much as the words. Do you recognise yourself in any of them? Or perhaps someone you know? Or just maybe you attended one of the events they were taken at. Thank you to all the photographers for their wonderful efforts down the years, not least Roger Elliott, Richard Coombs and Pete Brown.

I hope you enjoy this personal indulgence. I hope too that this book jogs some wonderful memories. Acts that have graced the stage at the City Hall, include The Beatles and David Bowie, Salisbury Amateur Operatic Society's excellent productions (now known as Musical Theatre Salisbury), and of course there have been the endless round of top notch comedians, including Jimmy Carr, Jethro, Stilgoe and Skellern, Ken Dodd, Jasper Carrott et al. And let's not forget the endless round of wrestlers, superstars of the Seventies.

Whatever your age or generation, this book should hold some memories for you. Enjoy!

James McCarraher.

"The ultimate success of the Hall will be gauged rather by the extent of its use than by its income and expenditure account."

Alderman Francis Moore

January 1963

"Perhaps it doesn't do anything absolutely perfectly but it does a lot of things only marginally imperfectly."

David Rawlinson

October 1989

PUTTING YOU IN THE PICTURE

"With a low façade in red and multi-coloured brickwork, the new building bears definite touches of Dutch styles, and is a dignified addition to the well-known architectural beauties of the Wiltshire city."

Kinematograph Weekly

It was on 11th December 1916 that Albany Ward Theatres Limited, a West Country cinema chain, opened a 514 seat cinema in Fisherton Street called the Picture House. At the time, there was a rush to open new cinemas due to the popularity of early silent film, and as a result, all sorts of strange and wonderful venues were utilised. In this case, the chosen location had up until its conversion enjoyed life as a Methodist Chapel.

Albany Ward was an ambitious man who had built up a small but thriving chain of cinemas based predominantly in Somerset and

Wiltshire. However, he was competing in a highly competitive market and by 1929, his company had become a small part of the vast empire of the Gaumont-British Picture Corporation.

Gaumont-British was in direct competition with its nearest rival, Odeon, for the biggest slice of this fast-expanding market. In Salisbury, the company was acutely aware that the Picture House was not big enough to sustain its share of the local market, so set about searching for a new site upon which a theatre could be built, this time to their own design and high specification, with ample capacity to meet local needs and turn a handsome profit.

They did not have to look far. The large timber yard, just a few doors along from their existing Picture House in Fisherton Street proved to be the perfect site. It was on a busy road, only a short walk from the town centre, and was easily accessible to the population of the City.

The timber yard was actually too small to accommodate the new building, so Gaumont-British purchased a sizeable chunk of the back garden to the adjoining Angel Hotel, giving them a plot big enough to realise their architect's dream.

The purchase of the land was completed on 18th September 1936 and the clearance of the area began. Little time was wasted in the construction of the building and by the following year, it had been completed.

The new cinema was of a rectangular shape and such was its size that it dwarfed the neighbouring shops and the prominent Angel Hotel. Externally, the new building's greatest feature was the very attractive Art Deco frontage framed by twin brick pillars topped with ornate towers. Three flag poles adorned the roof, giving the building a stately appearance. Kinematograph Weekly magazine described the frontage in the following manner:

"With a low façade in red and multi-coloured brickwork, the new building bears definite touches of Dutch styles, and is a dignified

addition to the well-known architectural beauties of the Wiltshire city."

The last part of the sentence is an interesting statement because it is fair to say that the style of the building failed to complement some of the older buildings in the city. That said, its brick frontage suited (and still suits) Fisherton Street and made an imposing addition to Salisbury. However, like most cinemas of the era, little attention was paid to the back or the sides of the building.

Patrons passing through this unusual entrance found themselves in a long vestibule which housed the box office. The floor was lavishly carpeted in a terrazzo design and the walls were painted in various shades of fawn, blue and silver. Settees and palm trees added to the comfortable and palatial atmosphere creating a decadent and somewhat exotic ambience.

The vestibule in turn led to the lavishly decorated foyer. The walls were elegantly veneered in wood and the whole effect was finished in friezes of daffodil yellow and apple green with the odd touch of silver. If you looked above your head, your eye would have been drawn to the panelled glass and architecturally interesting stepped ceiling which housed the lighting fixtures.

Three doors led from the foyer into the spacious auditorium which was built in a style known as 'the stadium design' with banked seating to the rear. This design was chosen with economy in mind; the construction of a balcony would have added considerably to the cost of construction and may possibly have resulted in a reduced capacity over all.

The walls of the auditorium were panelled in rich, warm tones of peach, relieved with lemon yellow, green and silver, each panel terminating in a rose-tinted dado rail. The ceiling was painted in similar colours to complement the effect and was crowned with an ornamental light fitting. Silk curtains lined the walls at intervals and the ceiling was painted in the same colour as the walls. The stage and screen curtains, also made of silk, in peach and cream with green and gold trimming, complemented the décor throughout.

The whole auditorium was designed to give the customers a feeling of warmth and comfort. At the time, many people lived with few home comforts or luxuries, so the cinema was a way of escaping the harsher realities of life. Visitors could kill an afternoon or evening and lose themselves in surroundings they could never hope to match in their own living room. It also has to be remembered that Salisbury is located within a rural area, so a trip to the pictures was one of the few affordable luxuries open to many people. It even had free parking at the adjoining Griffin's Court and a public pay 'phone!

The design of the building and particularly the frontage were without doubt a tremendous tribute to the talents of the three architects, William Edward Trent, his son William Sidney Trent and R.C.H Golding.

Trent Senior played a major part in designing the buildings that helped to make up the Gaumont-British Empire (though sadly, the majority have now since been closed down or bull dozed). He was an architect with an eye for detail, who was keen to ensure that his buildings were in every way fit for the purpose they were intended and strived for improvements with each new design.

By September 1937, the new building was ready to meet its public, erected and completed to a high specification by McLaughlin & Harvey, Ltd, General Contractors of Highbury Grove in London.

OPENING DAY

"I am sure you will agree with me that this is a wonderful theatre…"

Nova Pilbeam

The first staff photograph which features George Howes (centre of first seated row), Chief Projectionist Len Adams (back row, third from right), Second Projectionist Dave Watson (back row third from left).

On 18th September 1937, the original Picture House closed its doors as a cinema for the last time. However, it did not spell the end for this charming building. It found a new life as a warehouse before being taken over by the Army as a drill hall, then ENSA took over the building for entertainment purposes (Entertainments National Service Association, set up in 1939 to entertain the troops during the Second World War).

Local people will remember the building as the original Playhouse Theatre which served the City in this capacity from 1946 until its closure and replacement with a new, modern building in 1976. Actors and patrons recall this building with great affection. It was cramped, damp, the dressing rooms were hopelessly small, but it was still much loved for its quirkiness. It hosted a steady flow of repertory theatre companies and played a small but significant part in making stars of the likes of Kenneth Williams and Christopher Biggins.

Nine days after the closure of the original Picture House, Gaumont-British proudly unveiled to the public its latest pride and joy, imaginatively naming it 'The New Picture House', which boasted a capacity of 1,311 seats.

Opening day, 27th September 1937, had a carnival atmosphere with crowds queuing five abreast as far as Chapel Place on one side and Phillips Court on the other; everyone wanting to catch a glimpse of the V.I.Ps arriving and hoping to get a seat for the opening film, 'King Solomon's Mines' starring the wonderful singer and actor, Paul Robeson. The film was to be preceded by a Mickey Mouse cartoon, giving Walt Disney the honour of having the very first public screening at The New Picture House.

Salisbury resident, Sylvia Weston, remembers the day very well:

"At that time, my husband Dave had been appointed Second Projectionist. As the spouse of a member of staff, I was entitled to a free pass for the opening night which allowed me to sit in the special seats. However, when Dave went off to work, he forgot to leave my pass behind so I had to join the long queues outside and take my chance with everyone else. Thankfully, I managed to gain admission, but I had to pay!"

By 7.30 p.m. the 'House Full' boards were put up by the doormen. Those remaining outside gathered around the front entrance to watch the guests arrive.

The trumpeters of the 12th Royal Lancers played as the Right Honourable The Countess of Radnor, six Gaumont-British 'starlets' and the star of the evening, actress Nova Pilbeam, were escorted into the vestibule (more on Nova Pilbeam later). The scene was reminiscent of an opening night in the West End and received national coverage in the press.

Also present on the night were Mr Ecles, the Area Advertising Manager, Mr and Mrs C. Scammell who were the Deputy Mayor and Mayoress of Salisbury at the time, together with other local dignitaries.

It is worthy of a mention that both William Sidney Trent and William Edward Trent, the architects of the building, were also present.

Addressing a packed auditorium, J.D. Saunders, the Circuit Supervisor, introduced the new theatre to the people of Salisbury. He said that it gave him great pleasure to attend the opening ceremony of the new theatre and thanked the audience on behalf of the directors of the Gaumont-British Picture Corporation, for giving The New Picture House a good send-off. He had one regret, and that was that the Mayor of Salisbury was unable to be with them owing to a previous engagement and the Mayor had asked him to express 'his regret' [the original City Hall book stated that the Mayor had been in attendance, which had been inaccurately reported in certain historical publications]. Mr

Saunders pointed out that his company had had the pleasure of providing entertainment for the people of Salisbury for more years than he could remember, and he was very quick to point out that the gentleman who opened their very first cinema in Salisbury was in the audience. The gentleman concerned was none other than Mr Albany Ward, proprietor of the original Picture House in Fisherton Street, who received a warm round of applause.

Mr Saunders went on to say that the closure of the old Picture House had caused a tinge of regret in the hearts of the regular patrons, but they knew that today the picture-going public demanded something much better than the old Picture House could offer. His company, realising that demand, had erected a new theatre which he was quite sure would meet with their approbation (approval). Mr Saunders also introduced the Manager, Mr G.A. Howes, who had been handed responsibility for The New Picture House.

George Howes (pictured over the page) was an experienced Manager who had previously served as Assistant Manager at the

Kings Cross cinema before managing cinemas in Dorchester, Swindon and Frome.

There then followed speeches from Major Robson MP and Nova Pilbeam, who was presented with a bouquet by a young girl called Betty Street. The building was then officially opened by the Countess of Radnor, who expressed her pleasure at being asked to open such a fine theatre. In her opening speech, she declared that:

"...she felt sure that The New Picture House would not only serve Salisbury but also the outlying villages and that the perfect

photography, good sound and ideal conditions of the cinema would establish it as a popular house for entertainment."

Presentation to Nova Pilbeam by Betty Street.

Nova Pilbeam also made a speech that night, receiving a very warm welcome from the audience:

"I am very glad to be here tonight for this gala performance, and may I thank you for the wonderful reception you have given me. This is the first time I have been to Salisbury and during my short stay here I have been greatly impressed by the wonderful

Nova Pilbeam and Lady Radnor

buildings. I am sure you will agree with me that this is a wonderful theatre, and I think Salisbury is lucky to have such lovely buildings as this and the Gaumont. I wish this theatre the very best of luck."

Strangely, Nova Pilbeam and Lady Radnor only watched the start of the film before being escorted to The Gaumont Palace in New Canal (now the Odeon) at around nine o'clock. A huge crowd greeted and cheered them outside The New Picture House.

At the Palace, they both addressed the audience from the stage before returning to their seats in the upper circle at The New Picture House to see the end of the film.

At the end of the programme, Nova was driven off in a car, waving to the crowds as she left the City.

Nova Pilbeam

The New Picture House became an overnight success, competing with the Regal in Endless Street and the Gaumont Palace. Its popularity owed much to the luxury and comfort of the surroundings as it did to the superb and varied selection of films supplied by the chain at the time. As an added bonus, the cinema's stage provided the opportunity for live entertainment.

Under the guidance of George Howes, The New Picture House was in fine shape to face the challenges and demands of a film-hungry pre-war audience.

Before moving on to the war years, the guest of honour deserves a special mention. Nova Pilbeam is no longer a household name but in 1937, her visit to Salisbury was greeted with tremendous excitement. In terms of equivalent modern-day celebrities, she was very much an 'A List' star with huge drawing power.

Born in Wimbledon on 15th November 1919, Nova Margery Pilbeam first appeared on the stage at the age of five in an amateur production at Blackheath directed by her father, Arnold Pilbeam. Seven years later, having studied dance and elocution, she won her first big role as Marigold in 'Toad of Toad Hall'.

Aged just fourteen years, she made her film debut in the 1934 film 'Little Friend' about a girl who is driven to attempt suicide by her parents' proposed divorce. Although the picture was considered to be somewhat stilted, she made the great leap to fame overnight and in the same year appeared in her second film, Alfred Hitchcock's 'The Man Who Knew Too Much'. Variety magazine described it thus:

"A natural and easy production which runs smoothly and has the hall mark of sincerity."

The release of her third film, 'Tudor Rose', in 1936 saw her co – starring alongside John Mills, Sybil Thorndyke, Desmond Tester and John Laurie of Dad's Army fame. Many believed that the performances in her first three films were the best of her career.

Her first film as an adult star came in 1937, the year she attended the opening of The New Picture House, when she appeared in 'Young And Innocent,' another Hitchcock film, which was reputedly the director's favourite of all his pictures. The story, about an unjustly accused man helped by the chief constable's daughter, is a delightful and lighthearted chase tale. Nova and co-star Derrick De Marney are ideal screen partners.

Such was her involvement with the world of Alfred Hitchcock, that in 1939 she married his Assistant Director, Pen Tennyson (a Great Grandson of Alfred Lord Tennyson) but she was tragically widowed in 1941 when he died in a plane crash.

Nova branched out into television and theatre during her acting career and although she continued to make films up until 1948, her acting style arguably failed to move with the times.

Retiring from acting, she married the BBC Radio Journalist Alexander Whyte and started a family, having achieved more in thirty years than most people of that generation would hope to cram into a lifetime.

Nova is known to be a private individual, giving very few interviews. At the time of going to print, she is still with us, living a quiet life in Highgate, London.

Her filmography can be found at the back of this book.

THE PROGRAMME

PICTURE HOUSE
FISHERTON STREET, SALISBURY

Directed and Controlled by the GAUMONT-BRITISH PICTURE CORPORATION LTD

SOUVENIR OF THE OPENING
Monday, 27th Sept., 1937 at 7-30 p.m.

OPENING CEREMONY BY

The Right Honourable
The Countess of Radnor

The Directors of the Gaumont-British Picture Corporation Ltd, extend to you a hearty welcome to the Picture House and ask your acceptance of this Souvenir Programme.

OUR GUEST

*from the
Gaumont-British
Studios . . .*

Miss
Nova Pilbeam

Probably no newcomer to the Screen has aroused so much interest as did Nova Pilbeam, when in 1934, a schoolgirl of fourteen years of age, she made her film debut in "LITTLE FRIEND."

Nova's sensitive portrayal of a very difficult role brought her much deserved praise and although her appearances on the screen—in the two later films, "THE MAN WHO KNEW TOO MUCH" and "TUDOR ROSE"—have been all too infrequent they have, at least, given us the unique opportunity of watching the progress of one so talented and versatile, successfully merge into such a complete artiste that only maturity and further experience can improve her.

Her characterisation of Lady Jane Grey in Robert Stevenson's moving and beautiful "TUDOR ROSE," still a cherished memory of picturegoers in Salisbury, "made" her in America, but it was no more decisive than her stage success a few months later in London—in "THE LADY OF LA PAZ," in which she appeared by courtesy of "Gaumont-British."

The success of "LA PAZ" (which was by no means her first experience or association with the stage) and a period of study kept Miss Pilbeam out of the studios for sixteen months. Then Alfred Hitchcock decided to give Nova, now seventeen, her first adult role in "YOUNG AND INNOCENT." The film, a crime and escape story with a love-and-duty theme is just finished and "Hitch" is confident that his experiment has succeeded.

PICTURE HOUSE   SALISBURY

FOREWORD.

BRITISH enterprise and British labour have given Salisbury, through the Picture House, a luxurious addition to the amenities of the City, which should become a favourite rendezvous for those who wish to spend their leisure hours amidst pleasant surroundings.

In 1936 the Directors of the GAUMONT-BRITISH PICTURE CORPORATION following their progressive policy of bringing their existing theatres up-to-date, decided that the old Picture House, in Fisherton Street, had fulfilled its period of usefulness as a place of entertainment, and there being no facilities to extend, another location had to be found.

They were fortunate in obtaining a large site close by, behind the then existing Angel Hotel in Fisherton Street. Whilst doubtless many will regret the passing of the old Picture House, which has had a long and successful career (and even a place of amusement can have much sentimental regard attached to it), there are so many advantages in the new theatre, representing as it does the last word in modern construction, that it should enjoy still greater popularity.

The Directors are indebted to the Members and Officials of the Salisbury City Council for the unfailing courtesy and valuable co-operation and assistance which have at all times been extended during the construction of this Theatre.

The Directors and Management also take this opportunity of thanking the public of Salisbury and putting on record their deep appreciation of the wonderful support afforded their various enterprises over a period of many years.

The erection and completion of a modern picture theatre is a very specialised and complicated matter, and from start to finish it is the result of enthusiastic teamwork on the part of all concerned. MR. W. E. TRENT, F.R.I.B.A., F.S.I., Chief Architect of the Corporation, MR. W. S. TRENT, F.R.I.B.A., and MR R. C. H. GOLDING, are responsible for the planning, design and superintendence during building. The whole of the Engineering and Electrical work has been done under the direction of MR S. HART, M.I.E.E., the Company's Chief Engineer. The General Contractors were MESSRS. McLAUGHLIN & HARVEY, and General Foreman, MR. G. GRATWICK.

The foundations were constructed by FRANKI COMPRESSED PILE CO., LTD., 39 Victoria Street, London, S.W.1.

FOR YOUR ENTERTAINMENT.

The sponsors of this theatre, THE GAUMONT-BRITISH PICTURE CORPORATION, already control over 350 of Great Britain's leading cinemas, and are, therefore, in the unique position to acquire for presentation in Salisbury, the pick of the world's best pictures. *British film productions will always be given a prominent part in the programmes.*

The entertainment to be provided henceforth can best be judged by the programme to be presented here to-day, which shews the high standard which has been achieved and which it will be the promoters' earnest endeavour to maintain.

SCREEN PROJECTION.

Much attention has been given to the screen, the type selected assuring perfect reproduction of the pictures, and they will be projected by machinery which is the last word in efficiency.

PICTURE HOUSE   SALISBURY

YOU CAN HEAR.

At the Picture House the miracle of "Duosonic," a remarkable new system is employed. With "Duosonic" every member of the audience hears a perfect recreation of the original, completely intelligible, completely natural.

FOR YOUR SAFETY.

The building is a fire-resisting structure and all the stringent regulations laid down by the Cinematograph Act and the Licensing Authorities have been adhered to. Exits are numerous and adequate, and in a case of emergency, the entire Cinema could be emptied in less than 2½ minutes.

FOR YOUR COMFORT.

The seating is of the most luxurious type, with super sprung seats and deeply curved backs. Ample room is afforded and every seat commands an uninterrupted view of the stage and screen.

THE ENTRANCE HALL

The Theatre is equipped with a very efficient heating and ventilating installation, which will ensure a pure and healthy atmosphere at all times, as well as maintaining an even temperature.

FOR YOUR CONVENIENCE.

The convenience of patrons has been studied in every detail. Ample crush hall accommodation, waiting rooms and a Free Car Park are provided.

The provision of direct telephone communication from the auditorium to loud speakers in the pay-boxes reduces to a minimum the delay in filling empty seats when a queue is waiting.

THE STAFF.

Every member of the staff has been carefully selected and trained to give personal satisfaction to everyone who enters the theatre.

THE MANAGEMENT

is in the capable hands of MR. G. A. HOWES, and patrons will always receive the courtesy and great consideration for which he has been noted throughout his career.

A Description of the New Picture House

MARK OSTRER, Esq.
*Chairman and Managing Director,
Gaumont-British Picture Corporation Ltd.,
and Associated Companies.*

Modern in design and conception the front elevation, executed in red multi-coloured brickwork, with slender stone dressings, shows traces of Dutch influence. Over the main entrance, flanking a brick panel containing the name of the theatre outlined in neon lighting, are two circular towers, carried out with very ornamental brickwork.

It will be observed that the general advertising essential for a building of this kind has been designed to conform with the architectural features of the frontage, and together with the brightly coloured canopy and the brilliantly lighted exterior, clearly denote the house of entertainment.

Knowing that you are more concerned with what is happening inside, let us proceed into the building.

Passing through the wide swing doors, the Vestibule, with the illumination of its star-shaped electric light fitting reflecting on the brightly coloured terrazzo floor, presents an appearance at once cheerful and inviting. On entering the Entrance Hall we find an apartment 50ft. long by 30ft. wide, which gives ample room for patrons to circulate, and affords a spacious lounge wherein we may, if necessary, pause awhile in comfort to await a friend. Here a pay-box and chocolate kiosk are placed for our service.

The decorations though restrained are dignified ; the varying shades of fawn, blue and silver of the walls, harmonising with the rich tones of brown and blue in the carpet, combine to create a definitely pleasing atmosphere.

Having paid the modest sum demanded for admission, we pass into the Foyer, where the manager's office, telephone and cloak-rooms are placed. Here the decorations have received more elaborate treatment. Above the walls, which are covered with veneered wood applied in a diamond pattern, tones of daffodil yellow and apple green, together with a lavish display of silver, form a pleasing contrast. The ceiling rises in graceful steppings to the centre, and is panelled in five bays, each containing a glass lay light similar to those in the entrance hall, designed and produced by F. H. PRIDE, LTD., of 69-81 Clapham High Street, London, S.W.4.

Here, again, the floor is richly carpeted, and the whole scheme is suggestive of comfort and luxury, and imparts a feeling of pleasant anticipation of the surprises awaiting us in the theatre.

From the foyer we pass through one of the three doors into the Auditorium, which has 1,300 seats, 450 in the circle and 850 in the stalls. W. W. TURNER & Co., LTD., Birmingham, were the furnishers of the theatre.

The theatre, which is of the Stadium type, has a sense of spaciousness which it would be difficult to improve upon, the warm tones of the decorations have given it at the same time an impression of warmth and intimacy often lacking in a hall of such dimension, and this impression is still further emphasised by the skilful disposal of illumination from the electric light fittings on the walls and ceiling.

The colours ranging from various tones of peach relieved with lemon yellow, green and silver are carried over the ceiling and down the walls and with the deep rose of the dado merge into the rich red covering of the seats and carpets. The side walls are hung at intervals with silk curtains of colours to match the surroundings.

ELECTRICAL INSTALLATION.

A close-up view of a projecting room in a Gaumont-British Theatre showing on the left Gaumont Magnus Projectors and B.A. "Duosonic" equipment—on the right the Power Amplifier rack.

Patrons may judge for themselves the undeniably artistic value of the lighting throughout the theatre, to which very careful thought and investigation has been given, in order that the result may be adequate, not only from the point of view of illumination, but also that it may be pleasing and restful to the eye. They can judge also the first class picture which they see on the screen, the result of careful research work to find the correct combination of screen surface and projector with its attendant light source, which will faithfully portray the work of the camera.

But they may not realise the vast amount of machinery and equipment which is hidden "behind the scenes," and which, in the opinion of the Corporation's engineers, is essential to the efficient staging and maintenance of a first-class programme.

The Electrical Installation has been ably carried out by Messrs. A. Anderson & Son, of Middlesbrough, with local labour, in accordance with specifications of the Corporation's Chief Engineer, Mr. S. Hart, M.I.E.E., assisted by Mr. R. T. Dealey (Projection Plant) and Mr. W. F. Peerless (General Installation).

All essential equipment is duplicated, thus avoiding the risk of interruption in the programme. Particularly is this so in regard to the Projection Chamber, which is fitted with the latest machinery using Gaumont Magnus Projectors (with auto-fed high intensity arcs), which have been supplied by Gaumont-British Equipments Ltd.

Electricity is taken from the Salisbury Electric Light and Supply Company, Ltd., 400 volts for power and 230 volts for lighting. A high efficiency Westinghouse Metal Rectifier is provided for conversion of the public alternating supply to suitable direct current for feeding the arc lamps in the projectors.

The possibility of a temporary failure of the town supply plunging the theatre into darkness is guarded against by the provision of a large storage battery capable of supplying the lighting for a period of six hours.

The lighting fittings in the Auditorium were manufactured by Blunt & Wray, 70 Salusbury Road, Kilburn, London, N.W. 6., and the screen by H. V. Polley Ltd., 32 Shaftesbury Avenue, London, W.1.

ALL BRITISH SOUND.

The sound installation has been carried out under the direction of the Sound Section of the Engineering Department. "Duosonic," the new British Acoustic Sound System, the result of fifteen years extensive research, has been installed. "Duosonic" is the most up-to-date sound system in existence, and every improvement for range, balance and volume control, have been introduced, ensuring perfect distribution of sound to every individual in the audience. The power amplifier racks contain an output valve which dissipates 75 watts, at over 1,000 volts high tension.

FOR THE HARD OF HEARING.

Patrons whose hearing is defective will be pleased to know that the "Ardente" system has been installed. Separate earphones can be plugged into certain seats in the Auditorium and deaf people are enabled, by using these earphones, to regulate the volume of sound in accordance with their degree of deafness.

● THE NEXT PROGRAMME AT THE PICTURE HOUSE ●

Two Big Features

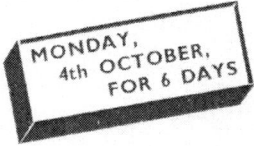

MONDAY, 4th OCTOBER, FOR 6 DAYS

Tom Walls

— AND —

Ralph Lynn

— IN —

FOR VALOUR

By BEN TRAVERS

Tom Walls as a convict kneading dough ; Ralph Lynn in similar capacity, scanning mailbags the former minus his moustache, the latter without his monocle—of such stuff are the Laughs made in "For Valour," the most hilarious comedy of the century. The Stars are not criminals all the time. Tom Walls will be seen as a wily financier, a fond father and a racing tipster ; Ralph Lynn, for film purposes, becomes a boy scout and a retired Army major ; but whatever their guise the comedy is the same. It is laughter, laughter all the way.

Ann Dvorak

— AND —

John Litel

— IN —

MIDNIGHT COURT (A)

Miss Dvorak plays the part of the court reporter who, one evening is horrified to see in the line-up the brilliant lawyer who was once her husband—but now a confirmed drunkard. The theme of the picture is her rehabilitation of him and the means by which they expose a gang of motor-car thieves.

John Litel—a favourite of the Broadway stage who is a recent convert to the screen—plays the part of the husband with sincerity and force.

The screen play was written by Don Ryan and Kenneth Gamet, the former having for years been the conductor of a column known as "Night Court" in a Los Angeles paper.

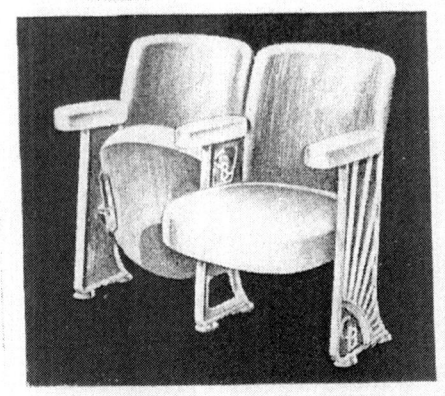

For your Comfort

For the comfort and enjoyment of patrons all the seats in the New Picture House were made and fitted by Turners of Northfield. Carpet-Laying was also entrusted to this firm of experts in Theatre furnishing.

THEATRE FURNISHERS

★ *Always invite a Tender from Turner*

W. W. TURNER & CO., LTD.
Station Road, Northfield, BIRMINGHAM

London Office: 28 NEWMAN STREET, W.1.
ALSO AT PARIS and GAND.

THE WAR YEARS

"I met Eddie in the theatre. He would come in and I showed him to his seat, but then he started talking to me and before I knew it he was outside waiting for me to walk me home."

Betty Bush, Usherette.

Upon the outbreak of war in 1939, every cinema in the country closed for one week. However, the Government soon realised that cinema would be a vital weapon in the propaganda war, keeping the public abreast of developments overseas as well as maintaining morale. Consequently, with the encouragement and support of Southern Command Headquarters, every effort was made to ensure that it was 'business as usual' with Gaumont-British Newsreels presenting 'The truth to the free people of the world.'

Locally, the job of bringing 'The truth to the free people of Salisbury' was not as straight-forward as it may have seemed. Gaumont-British only ever used to send one newsreel to Salisbury, which had to be shared between The New Picture House and its sister cinema, The Gaumont Palace. It was customary for the reels to be shown first at the Palace before being raced across town by the apprentice projectionist (and occasionally one of the usherettes) to The New Picture House. The poor lad (or lady) would often arrive exhausted and out of breath, sometimes with just minutes to spare. During the Fifties nothing had changed, other than this job had fallen to the main projectionist, as Bryan Rowe explains:

"Both cinemas had to share one copy of the Gaumont-British Newsreel. This one copy had to be collected from either cinema three times a day for showing well before the appropriate time. As I was the only member of the staff that biked to work it was normally my job to go and collect the newsreel in time for the

next screening in all weathers and heavy traffic! A large metal carrying case was provided for this exercise."

Many cinemas during the war suffered terribly from bomb damage, particularly in London, when one cinema after another was destroyed. Attendances were also heavily affected due to the sporadic and indiscriminate air raids which made it dangerous to go out at night.

The story was however very different in Salisbury. Whilst the City was not immune to bomb drops, The New Picture House and its rivals thrived. There was a very good reason for this. Within two weeks of the outbreak of war, ten thousand evacuees had flooded into the area from Portsmouth, a prime target during the war years because of its naval base.

As the war progressed, the American, Australian and Canadian forces moved in to the area, joining the already swollen population, making Salisbury a very busy and in many respects, cosmopolitan City during this era.

Many of these visiting service men took a shine to the local girls and on one such occasion, romance blossomed for New Picture House usherette, Betty Bush (pictured over page).

Betty caught the eye of a young GI called Edward Noack. Betty takes up the story:

"I met Eddie in the theatre. He would come in and I showed him to his seat, but then he started talking to me and before I knew it he was outside waiting for me to walk me home. But the thing was, my mother was there that night to walk me home. But after that, he came every night and he would walk me home. Then, when he got the army truck, he would drive me home, and I didn't mind that because it was so dark."

Eddie and Betty fell in love, married and Betty emigrated with her new husband. They stayed together until he passed away ten years ago.

Odstock Hospital on the outskirts of the City (now Salisbury Hospital) cared for many of the wounded soldiers during the war and they could often be found at The New Picture House watching the afternoon performances, where they were allowed in at a reduced rate.

Running a war time cinema was an important business and it was with this in mind that the Government of the day sanctioned a number of key posts as reserved occupations. For those of us too young to remember, a reserved occupation (also known as an essential occupation) is an occupation considered to be so important to a country that those serving in such occupations are exempt from military service. One of the big issues during the Second World War was propaganda and morale, hence the need to keep the cinemas going.

One such reserved occupation was the job of Chief Projectionist. This important role was filled by a popular man by the name of Len Adams, who was often simply known to friends and colleagues as 'Chiefy'. He was ably assisted by a Second and Third Projectionist.

Len (centre) and colleagues on the roof of the New Picture House

The Second Projectionist was a man by the name of Dave Weston, who not long after joining The New Picture House was promoted to Chief Projectionist at a Trowbridge cinema.

The Third Projectionist, the junior of the three as the title infers, was a young man called Ken Robson. Len and Ken became great mates and around the time The New Picture House opened, Len took his protégé to Olympia to see the world's very first television set. Both came away believing cinema was the best bet!

Unfortunately for Ken, his post was not senior enough to warrant his post as being classed as a reserved occupation and he soon found himself serving overseas helping the war effort.

Consequently, it would have been a relentless task for Chiefy to keep the two Magnus projectors running on his own, so he had some assistance from two female helpers. One was a lady by the name of Myrtle Penny and the other was a cinema Usherette by the name of Nora Jerrard. Both ladies played an invaluable role in keeping The New Picture House in business throughout the war years.

Len Adams and Ken Robson

Despite his considerable work load and the task of training his two new recruits, Len played his part in the war effort, joining the Home Guard and serving in the local fire watch. One of the key fire watch observation posts during the war was the roof of The New Picture House, which afforded a good view across parts of the City.

The shifts of the projectionists down the years could be gruelling. Whilst they often worked a five day week, a day could be from 9.30 a.m. to 11.00 p.m. It was not until the late Fifties that the average working day was divided into a split shift. Under the later system, staff worked either from 9.00 a.m. to 3.15 p.m. or 3.15 p.m. to 11.00 p.m.

Salisbury was fortunate during the war because it escaped most of the intense bombings that other locations suffered, not least Southampton and Portsmouth. Many believe that this was in part thanks to Salisbury Cathedral. The tallest spire in the Country was believed to act as a great navigation point for incoming German aircraft.

However, there was one particular day when the peace and quiet of Salisbury was shattered.

On Tuesday 11th August 1942, two German aircraft, believed to be Focke-Wulf Fw 190's (aircraft described as 'being armed to the teeth' – see picture) swept over Salisbury during the course of the afternoon and dumped their bombs on the railway line near Fisherton Street. Seven people were injured and damage was caused to many of the houses and shops in Fisherton Street. A hole was also made in the roof of the Old Manor and a scattering of shell cases sprayed across the grounds. Mr H.R.H. Witt, a local builder, had perhaps the luckiest escape. He was working in his office when the bombs fell. He took cover under his desk and as

the bombs dropped, the force of the explosions entirely demolished the building around him. However, most of the injuries and damage sustained were as a consequence of flying glass.

At the time of the bombings, The New Picture House was showing a double feature, the aptly titled 'One of Our Aircraft is Missing' and 'Weekend in Havana'. Sitting in the audience at the time was Walter Shobbrook, who had decided to take his Sister, Alice Ruby, to the pictures as a treat following his return from serving in Iraq.

It was during the early afternoon showing that events took a turn for the worse. War film enthusiasts may recall that 'One of Our Aircraft is Missing' depicts the escape of a British air crew from occupied Holland following the crash of their aeroplane. During the escape sequence, the airmen hide out in a harbour and under cover of an air raid, make their break for freedom.

The raid on Salisbury could not have been better timed if it had been planned, for as the audience watched the bombs drop on screen, Salisbury came under attack. Consequently, the cinema audience was offered a real-life soundtrack to their presentation as the cinema rocked, jumped and shook as one bomb after another fell on the City, causing chaos and confusion. Had they had 3D films at this stage in cinematic history, then the experience would have been complete!

The cinema management were aware of what was going on outside because the film was interrupted and the house lights were raised. Either manager George Howes or one of his staff ran down to the front of the stage shouting:

"It's alright, it's alright; they have all gone."

In typical British fashion, the lights were once again dimmed and everyone stayed to watch the rest of the film. Why let a few German bombs get in the way of a good picture?

The New Picture House was an enjoyable place within which to work. George Howes was a strong manager who ran a tight, but happy 'ship'. It reportedly had a great family atmosphere. Betty Bush recalls those days with fondness:

"It was nice, it really was and I really enjoyed it. It was just a nice place to work and all the girls got along so well."

George Howes was a man of tremendous character and great charm. He always addressed the usherettes as 'Missy'.

Despite this, the girls knew how to gauge his temperament by the colour of the suit he was wearing. It therefore followed that if he was wearing a brown pin-striped suit, he would be both amenable and approachable. By contrast, a black pin-striped suit let everyone know that he was a man with things on his mind!

Such was the standing of Mr Howes in the cinema community that in the latter half of 1946 he was promoted to Regional

Circuit Manager, giving him overall responsibility for the Gaumont-British cinemas in Salisbury, Swindon, Trowbridge, Chippenham and Frome.

George was replaced by Mr H.B. Walker, who had recently been demobbed from the Royal Navy, having served since May 1940. Prior to joining the Navy, he had managed the Gaumont-British cinema in Cirencester.

The management of the time was served by a busy and faithful staff that included a large-framed man by the name of Reg Blake. Reg served as the Cinema's Chief Doorman. Reg was in turn assisted by Roger Emm, David Stone and in later years by Roy Serviour. Reg also had a young lad who assisted him called Dennis, who used to act as his runner.

Reg and his colleagues could be regularly seen standing on the forecourt outside the main entrance of the building once everything was up and running for the day. Their job was to organise the queues (of which there were many) and deal with any queries. Like the top hotels, the doormen, resplendent in their smart uniforms and peaked caps added to the feeling of opulence and grandeur, creating a sense of occasion for the punters, whether the customer was there to see a George Formby feature or a Walt Disney 'classic'. It all helped to make a trip to the cinema something very special and a far cry from the average rural living room, with its poor furnishings and radiogram for company. Television of course, had yet to make an impact on the average household.

Picture – presentation of a gift by Page Dennis Corbin to Ken Robson and Beryl Wyatt on the occasion of their marriage. Featured from left to right:

Mr Close, Mr Allsop, Mrs Poolman, Mr J Adlam, Mrs Dowley, Mr H Dudman, Mrs Cooke, Mrs Thomas, Miss Brooks, Miss Muspratt, Miss Joliffe, Miss Fulkes, Ken Robson, Beryl Wyatt, Miss Andrews, Page Dennis Corbin, Miss Bell, Miss Parsons, Miss Adlam, Miss Hayter, Miss Emm, Mr Blake, Mr L Smith, Len Adams, Miss Hodgkinson, Mr Isaacs, George Howes and Mr E Hopkins.

Each day, the Usherettes would go on parade in the auditorium ready for inspection by the Manager, who would ensure that everyone was properly turned out. Torches were regularly inspected and Usherettes had to ensure that the front of the torch was always twisted to produce a sharp spotlight. Reg Blake was charged with looking after the batteries, arguably a position of power in a cinema!

The Usherettes regularly had to plead with him for new batteries when their torches began to fail.

The Chief Usherette was a lady called Muriel Burns (later to become Mrs Eldridge) and she would be tasked with reading out the rotas each day so that the Usherettes knew where they were supposed to stand. Once the girls were allocated their positions, they were prohibited from moving or swapping posts. The Usherettes also had strict guidelines to follow when showing patrons to their seats and it was considered a major faux pas to shine a torch directly into the face of a customer.

For an usherette, being placed for a shift in the stalls meant that they had to sit on seats that pulled down from the wall. A shift in the balcony guaranteed far more comfortable seating and for this reason, was often considered preferable.

Breaks in the shift were always welcome for the usherettes who often used to take turns nipping across to the Yorkshire Fisheries fish and chip shop in Fisherton Street.

Perhaps the worst job was the clearing up of the cinema between films, as Betty explains:

"When the movie was over and everybody left, then we would go round and clear out the ashtrays. I hated that job! But, it had to be done. I don't know if I ever did get used to the smoke but I never said anything."

Although the majority of the staff were the responsibility of the Management, the Projectionists were in many respects autonomous. They reported directly to the Area Engineer, a gentleman by the name of Mr Peerless, who was ably assisted by the Area Sound Engineer, Mr Best.

It wasn't always fun…

THE POST WAR YEARS

"If anyone steps on the British Lion's tail, it turns, and tonight, we are accepting the challenge which has been thrown out to us by the Americans."

Mr F. Sanders, Mayor.

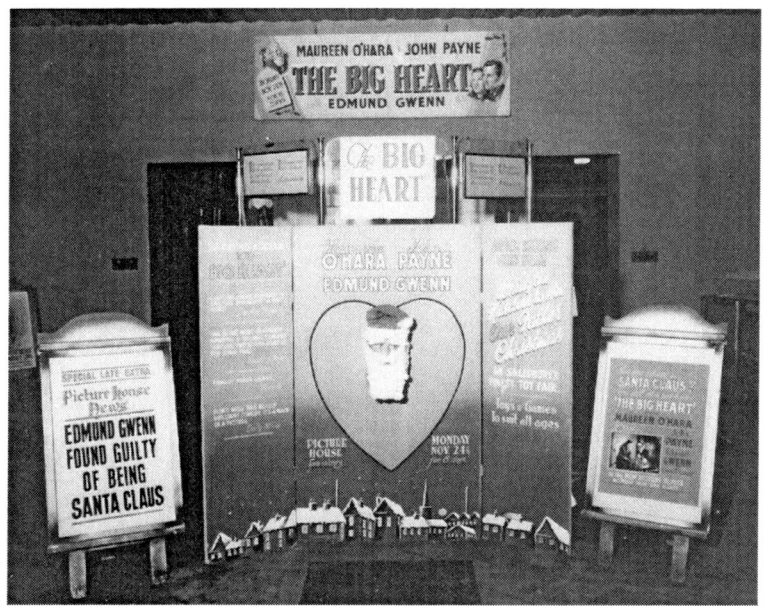

You may recall from the previous chapter that Len Adams ('Chiefy') was in charge of the projectors. However, he had lost young Ken Robson, his assistant, who had been called up during the war.

Assisted by Myrtle Penny and Nora Jerrard, he had kept the projectors rolling throughout this difficult time, helping to raise the morale of the local population, which included locally based soldiers and the evacuees.

In 1946, Myrtle and Nora graciously stepped down and Ken Robson gratefully returned to The New Picture House projection box. For Ken, returning to the cinema was not entirely alien as he had spent time overseas showing films to the forces. However, rather than returning as Third Projectionist, he was promoted to Second Projectionist and the third post was abolished. For young Ken, this was a massive bonus, which also meant that he received quite a substantial pay rise, much to his delight.

Len and Ken were a terrific team who worked well together. They were soon joined by a young apprentice who was given the responsibility of winding the films, checking the joins and ensuring that the reels were properly spliced in order to avoid any unnecessary breakdowns during a showing (never popular!)

Monday was always the day when the new reels would arrive for the week. They were always delivered by steam train to Salisbury station where the apprentice would be waiting with his wooden trolley (the reels were far too heavy for one man to carry). He would then tow his neatly stacked trolley back to The New Picture House where they would be offloaded and placed into the safe custody of Len or Ken, depending upon who was on duty at the time.

The checking of the newly delivered film reels was a laborious task. Often, the films arrived wound inside out, having always been shown at another cinema the previous week. These were the days when a limited number of prints of the film were made and cinema chains such as Gaumont-British were expected to revolve them around their circuit.

Once the reels were checked and corrected as appropriate, they were placed into numbered, sliding bins so that everyone knew in which order the reels had to be shown.

During the showing of a film, neither Len or Ken were allowed to abandon their post since the projectors needed constant monitoring and adjustment to ensure that the carbon arcs did not burn out.

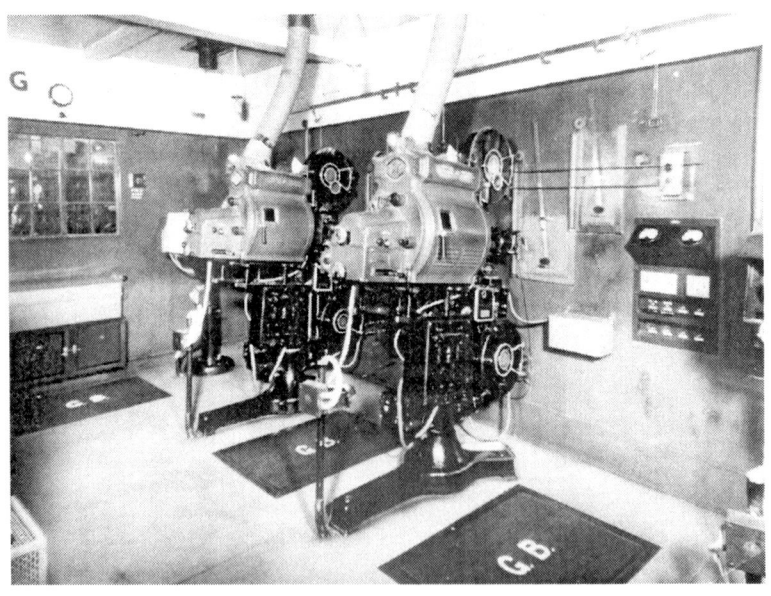

In those days, the biggest projectors often used what they called carbon arc lamps. Two carbon rods were connected to an electric power source. When the rods were pulled apart slightly, this produced a bright light, caused by the carbon particles burning between the points.

The projectionist had to keep a close eye on the carbon rods because they gradually became consumed, so they had to be regularly adjusted to maintain the correct distance between them, and the correct position relative to the optical centre of the lantern, during the showing of a film. In later years, this manual process was replaced by an automatic regulator….but for now, it was all very labour intensive. It also had to be remembered that the projectors from this era gave off a tremendous amount of heat, turning the Projection Room into a sweatbox!

As well as maintaining a close eye on the carbon rods, Len and Ken also had to watch out for breakages in the film. Whenever these occurrences arose, it has to be said that the decent people of Salisbury were generally good natured about it; there was rarely any chanting or booing!

The projectionists worked an average of a sixty hour week although the remuneration was good as Ken recalls:

"I recall taking home after the war the grand total of £6-15s on a good week although before the war this would have been nearer £3.00. But long hours meant that we were lucky to have one day off per week although sometimes this amounted to half a day."

Len loading a projector

Following the end of the War, the cinema was gradually settling down to a new normality. However, 1946 was a significant year – it was the year of the great flood!

On the evening of Sunday 23rd June, following a day of intense heat, a storm lying North-East of the City merged with another storm to the North, causing Salisbury's most catastrophic down pour in living memory. From about 7 p.m., over two inches of rain fell in as little as forty-five minutes causing flooding between eighteen inches and two feet deep. Castle Road and Castle Street were rendered impassable and a huge pool of water formed under Fisherton Street railway arch, stranding a coach on its way to Southsea, along with numerous private motor vehicles. In fact several hundred motor cars were stranded in and around Salisbury with flooded carburettors, causing lengthy traffic jams. In Catherine Street, a man twice fell flat on his back into the flooded road trying to push a stranded car, though it was all taken in good humour!

In The New Picture House, patrons were watching the latest double feature, 'Manhattan Music Box' and 'Come on Leathernecks', but the noise of the driving rain and ensuing storm rendered the soundtrack inaudible. To make matters worse and probably as a direct result of the river adjacent to Watery Lane overflowing, water began to cascade through the side doors of the cinema auditorium, forming a lake beneath the screen and flooding out the seats at the front. Some reports indicate that water may have come in through the foyer as well.

Despite the problem of the damp, the cinema remained open for business and while the children paddled in the pools of water, having fun squelching the soggy carpet, it was not long before the waters receded and staff could clear up the mess and return the building to normality once again.

During the War and the months thereafter, The New Picture House had enjoyed the benefit of Sunday opening courtesy of Defence Regulation 42B which was scheduled to remain in full force and effect, unless otherwise revoked, until 31st December 1947.

It was therefore down to the City Council to decide whether Sunday opening be banned once again, or that the status quo be maintained.

In modern times, the decision would have been a forgone conclusion, but during this era, the moral influence of the Church of England was far reaching.

The debate took great precedence both in the Council Chamber and occupied a great deal of space in the local press for many weeks to come. The local clergy threw down the gauntlet with the following statement:

"Remember the rest day is a fundamental law binding on all men, which can only be disregarded at peril."

The local clergy wanted the Council to hold a referendum on the subject but it soon became clear that they were in the minority, with not one single letter to Salisbury Journal coming out in outright support of the views of the local churches.

One person, T.M Broomgrove, writing to the paper, had a logical solution:

"May I suggest that the clergyman should hold later Sunday services, otherwise people are left to their own devices very early. Failing this let some enterprising clergyman attend the cinemas to conduct community hymn singing or hold a short service. One thing the Sunday cinemas have done is to keep their patrons interested and off the streets. It must be remembered that a number of people have few home comforts to hurry home to after the early finish of church services. Until the churches can offer something to take the cinemas' place, then it is my submission that they have no case for cinemas to be closed on Sunday."

The Rev. Mauleverer, who was the Vicar of St. Francis, took a pragmatic and modern view in his Parish Magazine. His view was that there was nothing wrong with Sunday football, golf, cinema or any other wholesome recreation for that matter, provided that the individual had first been to church. He did however stress that any trip to the cinema should be to see *decent* films!

These words of Broomgrove and the Rev. Mauleverer reflected the view of a great many local residents at the time. Sunday cinema had become a way of life for the people of Salisbury and the troops posted in the area, including a large Polish contingent. With not only economic but the social issues to consider, the choice to keep the cinemas open on Sundays was in many respects academic.

Despite the issue of Sunday opening resolving itself, storm clouds were amassing over the film industry. During the War years, American cinema had thrived, and much of Hollywood's income had come directly from British cinema audiences who craved the escapism it offered. In contrast, British cinema had suffered, with many of the films produced at home lacking the quality of pre-war releases. Consequently, many of the British films were married up with superior Hollywood films in order to get them into the picture houses up and down the country.

In 1947, Sir Stafford Cripps, the president of the Board of Trade, became extremely outspoken about the 'over-Americanisation of British culture'. The Board of Trade took measures against Hollywood. On 7 August 1947, an *ad valorem* tax (being a tax on personal property) of seventy five percent was placed on all future film imports. Foreign distributors were to pay three-quarters of the expected earnings on a film prior to its release in England.

Cripps was warned that the British film industry could collapse without the Americans but this fell on deaf ears. Hollywood retaliated in anger, boycotting the British market until the tax was lifted.

This all coincided with the British economy going through a massive slump.

Locally, there was defiance. Across the City at The Gaumont Palace, the Manager, Mr. R. M. Leddra was answering questions from the stage on the very subject.

It had been suggested to him by a number of patrons that the British film industry would shut up shop without the Americans pumping money into it.

"Stuff and nonsense" he declared!

Leddra spoke at length about there being a season of crises – there was the dollar crisis, coal crisis, food crisis and now they had a film crisis. He argued that the lack of American films actually provided British cinema with a golden opportunity to capitalise on this gap in the market and that British cinema would prosper. He was sure that the 'J. Arthur Ranks' of this world would not let us down.

The Mayor, Mr F Sanders, added his own comments to the debate:

"If anyone steps on the British Lion's tail, it turns, and tonight, we are accepting the challenge which has been thrown out to us by the Americans."

Mr Sanders was convinced that there was enough talent, energy and enterprise in the British film industry to ride out the crisis.

The truth of the matter was quite different from the rhetoric thrown out by the Manager and the Mayor. Britain needed the American blockbusters and despite Mr Leddra's faith in J. Arthur Rank, they actually turned over a loss as a consequence of the boycott. It was a very grim state of affairs.

The impasse between the British Government and Hollywood prevailed until 1948, when a settlement to the problem was reached and Hollywood once again sent their films over for the British public to enjoy.

Despite making losses, J. Arthur Rank had aspirations to merge the Gaumont-British chain with the huge Odeon chain, which had fallen under his control in 1941 following the death of its founder, Oscar Deutsch (for the younger reader, 'Odeon' stands for '**O**scar **D**eutsch **E**ntertains **O**ur **N**ation'). The Government had repeatedly resisted this move, so between 1948 and 1949, Rank formed a separate company to circumnavigate this ruling called Circuits Management Association Limited (C.M.A). This effectively controlled the running of both Gaumont-British and Odeon, bringing the two companies under the control of one organisation.

And whilst British cinema industry was going through turmoil and momentous changes, there was another surprise for the staff of The New Picture House, with the return of the highly popular George Howes to the helm. Furthermore, the cinema was now more than ten years old and the 'New' was duly dropped from its title. Whilst the staff were genuinely delighted at his return, it was short lived.

Gaumont-British were aware of his talents and promoted him to Manager of the more prestigious Gaumont Palace in New Street where he succeeded Mr Leddra as Manager.

When George Howes moved on, his Assistant Manager, Mr. Close took over as Acting Manager until a permanent replacement could be found.

In December 1949, Mr Close handed over to the new Manager, Charles Tappy. Charles had spent twenty-two years in service to Gaumont-British, starting as a film boy in the days of the silent films.

He had previously managed the Gaumont at Frome where he had been in charge for five years, so the promotion to a more prominent venue would have been a hefty leg up the promotional ladder. In turn, Mr Close took on his first full managerial role as Manager at Charles' old cinema.

The Forties had been a chaotic and tumultuous decade for British cinema and on a personal level, for The Picture House.

It therefore seemed fitting that the staff of the three local cinemas should come together for a joint party at the Assembly Rooms (now above Waterstones in the High Street) where everyone was entertained by our very own Rosemary Squire (who was at the very beginning of a sixty-plus year career in show business), closing the era on a positive note.

OSCAR DEUTSCH ENTERTAINS OUR NATION

"If they made a lot of noise, I only had to tell them once!"

Muriel Eldridge, Head Usherette.

As if the cinema had not seen enough turmoil in the previous decade, the Fifties began with more changes.

The first affected the staff in the projection room. Gaumont-British decided that it was time to replace the old Magnus Projectors with new GB Kalee projection equipment which was modern, far more efficient and a lot more pleasant for the Projectionists to operate.

This meant a certain amount of retraining and the staff had to learn new film lacing techniques and loops to ensure that there was constant synchronisation between the picture being shown on the screen and the soundtrack coming through the speakers.

The benefits of the new projectors were immediately apparent. They were much quieter than their predecessors and gave off much less heat. The old Magnus Projectors were virtually untouchable when they were running at their hottest.

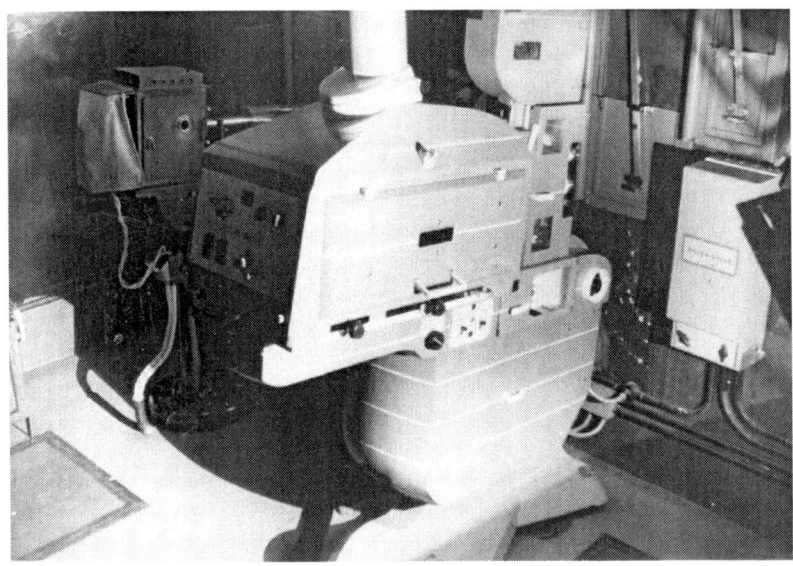

However, Fifties projectionist Bryan Rowe recalls that it was not as straight forward as it all seemed:

"The GB Kalee projectors were great to operate. The only downside was the Carbon Arcs which could create unpleasant fumes - this was especially if the weather outside was windy as you had to keep the arcs chimney flu closed as the draught would come down the chimney and cause the carbon flame to flicker which of course would affect the picture on the screen. The Odeon's projection box was quite small and if the weather was such that you couldn't open the outside door you can imagine how the fumes built up! I often wonder in our present times of

'Health and Safety' how the powers-that-be would have dealt with this.....a long way from the present Digital age."

However, the most significant change was a complete rebranding of The Picture House. In a rare and almost unprecedented move, Circuits Management Association Limited decided to transfer ownership of the cinema to the Odeon chain (remember, both Gaumont-British and Odeon were now owned by J. Arthur Rank). This only happened to one other cinema, the Angel at Islington.

This meant that the newly branded Odeon in Fisherton Street could now take Odeon film releases, placing them on a different film circuit to the Gaumont-British cinemas. On 27th February 1950, the old neon signs were removed from the frontage and the famous Odeon lettering was erected in its place.

There was however one old practice that continued beyond the days of the Picture House into the Odeon era, as Bryan Rowe explains:

"Up until 1956, Sunday programmes were always re-runs of classic older films from the Forties. These films were often in very poor condition, full of dodgy joins which had to be re-spliced by hand. Perhaps if the film was in a very poor condition some forty or fifty joins may have to be re-spliced often taking hours of work. Films arrived un-spooled and had to be carefully wound onto our spools. Often if a film had previously been projected through an old projector, it would arrive in an oily condition and have to be carefully cleaned off."

It was at about this time that the Old Picture House next door experienced a new lease of life when in 1951, it became the Salisbury Playhouse. Due to the high number of theatre productions, there was always call for music to be played and Len Adams and his team came to their rescue by lending them recordings from the Odeon's extensive archive, as Bryan elaborates:

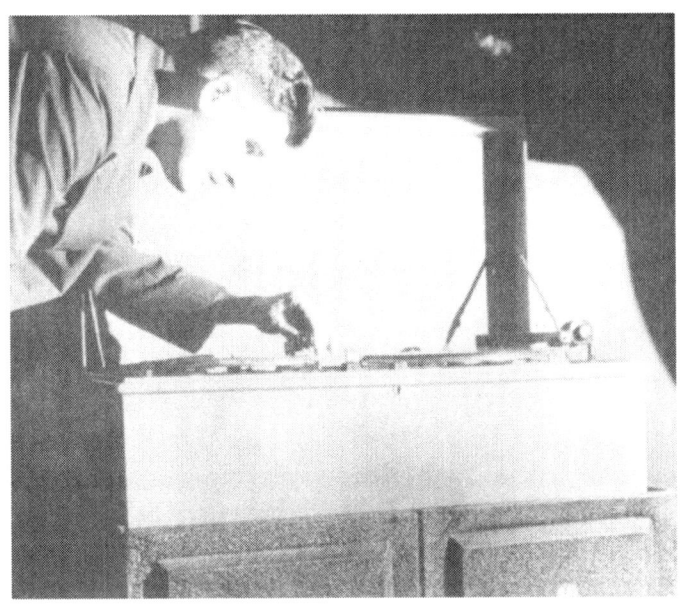

Len Adams operating the twin turntables

"All the music played during the intervals between films was played on 78 r.p.m records and later on LPs. We used to have to time records to coincide with the fade out of the censor title of each film. The Playhouse would often request specific titles for their plays and I remember loaning them a vocal version of 'Bless 'Em All' for their production of Willis Halls play 'The Long, The Short and the Tall'. The Playhouse started the careers of many film and television personalities including Leonard Rossiter and George Baker, who became a close friend of Len Adams."

Cinema in the Fifties was now starting to lose its appeal. Whilst during the Thirties and Forties it was an essential form of entertainment and in many respects, still something of a novelty with the arrival of the 'talkies', tastes were now rapidly changing. Live entertainment was making a big comeback and this, coupled with the growing popularity of television (the next big thing), it was putting the squeeze on cinema audiences. The Queen's Coronation on 2nd June 1953 particularly helped to popularise the sale of television sets. It was a bitter irony for Len Adams, who no doubt cast his mind back to the day he took a young Ken Robson to Olympia to see the first television set, that this medium would wreak such havoc on the industry he loved. Len genuinely disliked television.

Despite the downward trend, there was one area which remained popular with youngsters, which is still run in cinemas today. Saturday morning cinema had been founded in 1943. It started out as 'The Gaumont-British Junior Cinema Club' when the cinema was still known as The New Picture House. The Club cost six pence per show and attracted a staggering seven hundred to eight hundred children per week. Each week there was a quiz, with children being notified of the subject the previous week (for example history or geography). Prizes were awarded to the winners. It was also normal for there to be sing-a-longs, with Mrs Nugent on piano, or if she was unavailable, the children would sing along to a gramophone player. Typically, songs included 'Land Of Hope And Glory', 'You Are My Sunshine' and 'Bless You'. How times have changed…

The popularity of the Club spilled over into the Odeon era, though the format changed. And whilst the Regal in Endless Street ran a similar Saturday morning club, those who remember going to the local cinemas at the time testify to the superiority of the programmes shown by the Odeon in Fisherton Street.

Roger Godwin, whose family ran the Shoe & Leather business opposite the Odeon in Fisherton Street, was an avid fan of the Saturday morning cinema club, crossing the road with the entrance fee burning a hole in his pocket, looking forward to a wonderful morning of entertainment.

Many children stocked up with sweets at another Fisherton Street shop, run by the two Miss Ling (later to be owned by well-known local figure and future Mayor, Tom Cowie). The children would pay their entrance fee and be treated to two and a half hours of pure entertainment. A local lad at the time, Tony Curtis, remembers those days with great affection:

"The shows would usually consist of a cartoon, a short film, then a serialised programme such as Flash Gordon, which would run from week to week ensuring that we went back for more! After a short break came another cartoon and finally a full length feature film, such as a 'Lassie' movie."

It was not uncommon for local entertainers to come along and amuse the children between programmes and regulars included a local man called John Batt and Ralph Francis, the Punch and Judy man.

Saturday morning cinema could regularly be an ordeal for Usherettes who often found the experience traumatic, having to cope with missiles being thrown from one side of the auditorium to the other. One of the biggest scallywags was a young John Martin, who went on to represent the Wilton Ward on the now defunct Salisbury District Council.

Mrs Eldridge, Head Usherette (who confesses to attending Saturday morning cinema wearing curlers under her hat), was always kind but firm:

"If they made a lot of noise, I only had to tell them once!"

Betty Noack recalls her time as a Saturday morning usherette between 1945 and 1946 with some affection:

"We would have movies every Saturday morning so the kids could see them. They used to watch Roy Rogers, Gene Autry, different people like that; Western movies and funny movies. But the children were pretty good; I mean they sat in their seats."

In the latter days, perhaps the biggest scallywags of all were the Projectionists, as Bryan Rowe confesses:

"We used to have fun with the spotlights focused on the 'Ice Cream Girls' at the start of each interval...we would keep the spotlights trained on them for as long as possible so that it dazzled them and they found difficulty in adjusting to serving the long queue of expectant customers!"

Bryan also recalls the Saturday morning showings with some affection (and slight trepidation):

"The programme of films would be kept to a fairly strict formula...cartoon, comedy, The Three Stooges, Laurel & Hardy...a serial, Flash Gordon, Batman etc. then the main feature film. If, as often happened, there was not a lot of action in the feature film, all the kids would start talking and shouting out and the Usherettes would have to go up and down the rows shining their torches on the kids' faces to try to get them to be quiet. Before the actual film show the Duty Manager would come on stage to announce birthdays and have a general interchange of patter with the kids. Then there would be the point when the whole audience would join in the established chorus to the tune 'Blaze Away'. It went as follows;-

*'We come along on Saturday Mornings,
Greeting everybody with a smile,
We come along on Saturday Mornings,
Knowing it's well worth while,
As members of the Odeon Club we all intend to be,
The citizens when we grow up,
The champions of the free,
We come along on Saturday Mornings,
Greeting everybody with a smile, smile, smile ,
Greeting everybody with a smile.'*

Real shades of Post War patriotism here!"

However, the Saturday morning format had its dissenters, not least Miss G. A. Moore, the Headmistress of South Wilts Grammar School for Girls:

"I think it is a bad thing to make a habit of the Saturday morning cinema. Children will give up anything rather than their Saturday morning entertainment – Sunday School treats and visits to Bournemouth do not attract them…It is a commercial proposition and I can't think that it is for the good of the children. It seems an unnecessary waste of money and they are seeing things which are not of any good whatever."

With the high turnover of films passing through the cinema from week to week, there was always the problem of how to promote forthcoming features at short notice. 'Richard III', starring Laurence Olivier, prompted one member of staff to tie a large crown to the central flag pole.

Large external displays were often placed across the canopy and for one film, a huge parachute was dangled over the frontage to catch the eye of punters.

'The White Unicorn' (1947) & 'The Chiltern Hundreds' (1949)

The Browning Version (1951)

Competitions were regularly run and families were invited as guests if they had something in common with a particular film. For instance, Mr. and Mrs Scott of Endless Street and their five sons were invited to see a film called 'All My Sons'. It was a low cost gimmick, but raised the profile of the feature being shown, much in the same way that tickets are now given away during radio phone-ins.

Well known personalities connected with the films occasionally made a special appearance, including Jerry Desmonde, who visited Odstock Hospital whilst promoting 'The Cardboard Cavalier' accompanied by an Usherette dressed as Margaret Lockwood. Another visitor to Odstock was 'Uncle Remus', alias James Baskett who starred in the Disney classic, 'Song of the South'. Derrick De Marney visited the cinema to promote 'She Shall Have Murder' and answered questions from the stage.

Richard Todd ('633 Squadron') was another popular visitor though it is unclear what film he was promoting.

In 1961, almost exactly fifteen years after the great flood of 1946, Fisherton Street was again flooded, although the damage to the Odeon is unknown.

The gradual decline in audiences placed C.M.A in a position whereby it was becoming impracticable for them to keep their two Salisbury cinemas running in direct competition. This is borne out by projectionist Bryan Rowe's recollections of the time:

"The decline in cinema audiences in Salisbury, as television gained its hold meant that in the final months of the cinema, there were often as few as fifty people attending an evening performance. This was a very sad time as one recalled that in 1956 the cinema was packed for all performances for the British film 'Reach for the Sky'. Also one remembers a packed cinema for Rogers and Hammerstein's 'Oklahoma' which looked fabulous on the large cinemascope screen. I remember during 'Reach for the Sky', week-long queues stretching down Fisherton Street at one o'clock in the afternoon! During the final year or so of the Odeon's decline, austerity measures meant that the cinema's Doorman/Boilerman/Carpark Attendant were not replaced and Projection staff [which also included John Adlam, Dennis Lavender and Pat O'Meara] *in addition to their duties had to (on a daily basis) clean out, light and service the boilers throughout the day. We had to check the boilers regularly throughout each shift, between reels, to ensure there was no clinker build-up and also to refill the coke hopper feeds. In addition, we had to supervise the car park and switch on outside lighting etc. All this for no extra money!"*

In 1961, a decision was made to axe one of the cinemas.

Despite the luxurious surroundings of the Odeon in Fisherton Street, it was a foregone conclusion that it would lose out to its superior Sister in New Canal. The Gaumont Palace had history, architecture and a better location in its favour. How could the chain turn its back on the most beautiful cinema vestibule in the world, The Hall of John Halle? The Palace was beyond doubt the jewel in their crown.

Accordingly, on 30th December 1961, the last feature was shown for the final time. Just as the cinema had opened with a Disney feature (a Disney 'short' supporting 'King Solomon's Mines'), so it finished with another of their films, 'One Hundred and One Dalmatians'.

Of the twelve remaining staff, most were either laid off or found employment elsewhere within the City. However, Chief Usherette Muriel Eldridge and part time Usherette Yvonne Oliver were transferred to the Gaumont Palace along with the last manager of the era, Bill Case.

Muriel Eldridge remembers her last day very clearly:

"After the final performance, I caught the bus home with mixed feelings; in some way sad to see the Odeon close but looking forward to a fresh start."

So what was to become of the old cinema?

Read on!

A NEW HALL FOR SALISBURY

"The ultimate success of the Hall will be gauged rather by the extent of its use than by its income and expenditure account."

Alderman Moore.

So the Odeon in Fisherton Street was no more...

But as we all know, this was not the end of the story but the beginning of a new, long and exciting chapter in the history of the building, which was still just twenty-four years old.

Salisbury City Council had for many years since the end of the Second World War, been searching for a site to build a new

Memorial Hall in memory of those that had given their lives during the last two wars. The people of Salisbury had been steadily but generously contributing to the Salisbury Victory Fund for this very purpose.

The idea was to create a multipurpose community centre where residents could come together for a host of different events. A number of sites were looked at and considered by the City Council.

It seemed that a location in Castle Street had been firmly agreed upon, when C.M.A approached the Council with an offer to sell them the Odeon in Fisherton Street.

This was an offer that was ultimately too good to refuse. The Salisbury Victory Fund did not have enough in the 'pot' to buy the building and complete a full conversion outright, so the City Council dug deep into its own pockets and much to the delight of local residents, the building became public property.

There was however a covenant in the title deeds preventing the Council from showing films in the building, thus ensuring that it would never be in direct competition with The Gaumont Palace.

The building remained off limits to the public for over a year during the conversion until it was formally opened to the public on 2nd February 1963. The City Hall was born, at a total cost of £80,000 (£38,000 of which came from the Victory Fund).

However, the mantra of the City Council was clear. It was not about the money, it was all about the people as Alderman Moore pointed out:

"The ultimate success of the Hall will be gauged rather by the extent of its use than by its income and expenditure account."

Externally, the existing front entrance was used, with the old Odeon wording being removed and the City's crest being erected in its place. The grand canopy was re-clad with the building's new name emblazoned in lettering that left the public in no doubt that the City Hall had well and truly arrived!

It looked grand with its handsome doors and staircase leading to the upstairs rooms.

So, who could Salisbury City Council appoint to run this new venue? Who knew the building better than anyone else?

The answer was obvious. 'Chiefy'!

Len Adams was duly appointed the very first Manager of the City Hall, a post he held until his retirement in the early Seventies. To date, he remains one of the longest-serving members of staff at the venue.

It was not long before Len and his team were pressed into action, not as venue hosts but as good neighbours to the shop keepers in Fisherton Street. Roger Godwin takes up the story:

"In the early 1960's there was a serious fire in the Yorkshire Fisheries premises almost next door to us [the Shoe & Leather business]. *The then manager of the City Hall opened the front doors to myself and my father at 3a.m. to move stock across the road to safety in the event of the fire getting as far as our building. Fortunately, it did not quite reach us."*

Salisbury Amateur Operatic Society

The opening of the new facility was not without its teething problems. One of the main benefactors of the new hall was Salisbury Amateur Operatic Society (S.A.O.S) who had raised a considerable amount of money towards the Victory Fund total.

S.A.O.S had been around for a remarkable fifty years at this point and had staged countless productions at the old Picture House (then operating as the current Salisbury Playhouse).

The problem they faced was the small capacity of the Playhouse theatre. Over a theatrical run, they could draw in a maximum of three thousand patrons which was financially restricting. It ultimately meant that they were often working to tight budgets and had to be modest with their productions, staging the cheapest of musicals whilst hoping and praying for a full house.

The old Playhouse – then home to S.A.O.S

Those familiar with the old building will recall the problem with flooding. The orchestra pit was renowned for filling up with water during a production. As Joyce Bowden recalled with some amusement, whilst the orchestra were keeping time, the man on the stirrup pump was playing to another rhythm and tune, trying to stop the musicians from disappearing under the deluge of water!

Initially, the prospect of a new City Hall building in Castle Street had caused a major stir within the Society. The brand new hall had a planned capacity of 750 seats. Furthermore, the Council had invited the Society to contribute ideas for the new building so that it was perfect for staging their productions. S.A.O.S had even put aside £1,400 for the project. The net result would have been a building custom-built for their requirements.

The purchase of the Odeon in Fisherton Street consequently came as a great surprise and also something of a headache. On the positive side, the capacity of the City Hall was more than they could have dreamed off, coming in at just under a thousand seats, thereby enabling them to stage the most lavish and generous of productions. The downside was that the building had severe limitations for a theatre company that required a gigantean effort to overcome, not least the lack of wing space.

S.A.O.S went through a series of meetings with the City Council and put forward a list of ideas including an orchestra pit with covers, additional stage lighting directed from the auditorium and additional lines, pulleys and cleats for flying borders and back cloths.

These were carefully considered by the Council who turned down the orchestra pit due to the technical difficulty and expense, but additional lines were soon installed along with the requested lighting.

In December 1963, S.A.O.S staged their very first production at the City Hall. 'Oklahoma' was a triumphant success, despite the stage crew having to cope with six sets and limited space. They now knew that the City Hall would be their permanent home, but there was still room for improvement!

Further lines, paid for by the Council, were added to the stage the following year, rigged up by the husband of a Society member, who was a lumberjack, enabling them to stage 'Show Boat' (December 1964), with its ambitious fifteen scene changes.

The later addition of catwalks meant that the City Hall now had the stage, equipment and space to host the most ambitious of shows.

One of the major obstacles to S.A.O.S achieving their aims and ambitions was the fact that the new Hall not only served as a theatre, but doubled as a multi-purpose community venue (unlike the old Playhouse). Their theatrical aspirations were in direct competition with a host of events looking for a new home, not least the visiting pop stars, the gala balls and all-star wrestling!

Wrestling

Wrestling, whilst culturally at odds with Amateur Operatics, was in many ways just as theatrical! Who could top the drama of two or more men grappling in a ring battling for two falls, two submissions or a knockout?

Up until the opening of the Hall in 1963, wrestling in Salisbury had been hosted at the old Corn Exchange, which readers may know better as the main library at the bottom of Castle Street.

The City Hall proved to be the perfect home for a sport which had first hit our television screens in the Fifties and was now reaching a much wider audience courtesy of ITV's 'World of Sport', which began its run of one thousand and fifty episodes in the Summer of 1968.

There was a major interest in Salisbury for this most physical of contact sports and it would regularly attract six hundred plus punters at a time. The area is known for having a large gypsy population and they would faithfully turn out to boost the numbers alongside other locals.

Salisbury City Hall was fortunate enough to have the benefit of one of the top promoters in the country – Herbert Deveureux's Deveureux Promotions (later inherited by his son Charles). In truth, the local events were being hosted by top welterweight wrestler Ken Joyce under the Devereux banner.

CITY HALL SALISBURY

Devereux Promotions Ltd. Present

WRESTLING

SATURDAY, JAN. 16th 1965

Doors open 6.30 p.m.   Commence 7.30 p.m.

International Heavyweight Contest

THE EXECUTIONER
DE BETHUNE   The French Terror. Undefeated in 8 years wrestling

v

ROY BULL DAVIS
PLYMOUTH   Western Area Heavyweight Champion

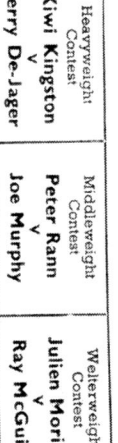

Heavyweight Contest	Middleweight Contest	Welterweight Contest
Kiwi Kingston v **Jerry De-Jager**	**Peter Rann** v **Joe Murphy**	**Julien Morice** v **Ray McGuire**

Luxury Seating At All Prices

Prices 10/6 : 8/6 : 6/6 : 4/6 : 3/-

ALL RIGHTS OF ADMISSION STRICTLY RESERVED

Advance Booking: TED HARDY TRAVEL AGENCY
24b Milford Street, Salisbury.   **Tel. 2670**

CAR PARK CASTLE STREET   LICENCED BAR APPLIED FOR

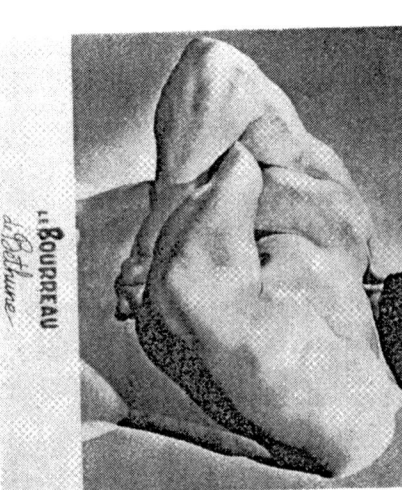

Le BOURREAU de Bethune

CITY HALL
Fisherton Street
SALISBURY
SATURDAY, APRIL 25th

Doors Open 6.30 p.m.　　　　Commence 7.30 p.m.

See The Stars of TELEVISION Wrestling Here
DEVEREUX PROMOTIONS LTD. proudly present

WRESTLING

WELTERWEIGHT CONTEST
THE ONE AND ONLY

MICK McMANUS
LONDON　Southern Area Welterweight Champion

v

Winner of Tournament on April 11th

LIGHT HEAVYWEIGHT CONTEST

Johnny KWANGO v Clayton THOMSON
WEST AFRICA　A Clever Wrestler　　　SCOTLAND　Light Heavyweight Champion

Welterweight Contest	Light Heavyweight Contest
JULIEN MORICE	**REG TROOD**
TOULOUSE, FRANCE	HAMMERSMITH
v	v
TONI SKARLO	**HARRY KENDALL**
ANGLO - ITALIAN	BRIXTON

Luxury Seating At All Prices　　ALL RIGHTS OF ADMISSION STRICTLY RESERVED

Prices　10/6 : 8/6 : 6/6 : 4/6 : 3/-

Advance Booking: **TED HARDY TRAVEL AGENCY**
24b Milford Street, Salisbury.　Tel. 2670

CAR PARK CASTLE STREET　　　　　　　　LICENCED BAR APPLIED FOR

CITY HALL
SALISBURY
SATURDAY, JANUARY 30th *1965*

Doors Open 6.30 p.m.   Commence 7.30 p.m.

See The Stars of TELEVISION Wrestling Here

DEVEREUX PROMOTIONS LTD. proudly present

WRESTLING

£100 INTERNATIONAL 8 MAN K.O. TOURNAMENT — 7 CONTESTS

Preliminaries, Semi-Finals and Final will take place the same evening.

Ken JOYCE

JEAN **CORNE** M/W Champion of France	REG **TROOD** HAMMERSMITH
BILLY **CATANZARO** TUNIS	KEITH **MARTINELLI** BOLTON
JOE **MURPHY** DUBLIN	KEN **JOYCE** European W/W Champion
IVAN **PENZECOFF** BOLTON.	PETER **SZAKACS** HUNGARY

Reg TROOD

Luxury Seating At All Prices   ALL RIGHTS OF ADMISSION STRICTLY RESERVED

Prices 10/6 : 8/6 : 6/6 : 4/6 : 3/-

Advance Booking: **TED HARDY TRAVEL AGENCY**
24b Milford Street, Salisbury.   Tel. 2670

CAR PARK CASTLE STREET   LICENCED BAR APPLIED FOR

CITY HALL
Fisherton Street
SALISBURY

1964

SATURDAY, NOVEMBER 7th

Doors Open 6.30 p.m.　　　Commence 7.30 p.m.

See The Stars of TELEVISION Wrestling Here

DEVEREUX PROMOTIONS LTD. proudly present

WRESTLING
DOUBLE MAIN EVENT

International Heavyweight Contest

STEVE VEIDOR v RAYMOND NAPOLITANO

SALISBURY'S FAVOURITE　　　　　　Tough American from Charlotetown

Heavyweight Contest

PRINCE KUMALIE v HENRI PIERLOT

West African Warrior　　　　　　　　　　ANGLO-FRENCH

CORTEZ BROS. v TOUGH GUYS

WELTERWEIGHT CONTEST

PETER CORTEZ v PETER RANN

DULWICH　　　　　　　　　　　　　　LONDON

MIDDLEWEIGHT CONTEST

JON CORTEZ v JOE MURPHY

DULWICH　　　　　　　　　　　　　　DUBLIN

Luxury Seating At All Prices　　ALL RIGHTS OF ADMISSION STRICTLY RESERVED

Prices 10/6 : 8/6 : 6/6 : 4/6 3/-

Advance Booking: TED HARDY TRAVEL AGENCY
24b Milford Street, Salisbury.   Tel. 2670

CAR PARK CASTLE STREET　　　　　　　　　LICENCED BAR APPLIED FOR

CITY HALL
Fisherton Street
SALISBURY

1964

SATURDAY, JULY 18th

Doors Open 6.30 p.m.   Commence 7.30 p.m.

See The Stars of TELEVISION Wrestling Here

DEVEREUX PROMOTIONS LTD. proudly present

WRESTLING

TERRIFIC HEAVYWEIGHT CONTEST

THE FAMOUS MASKED   PETER FAMEME

ZEBRA KID   v   MAIVIA

COLUMBUS, U.S.A. 20 Stone   PAGO-PAGO SAMOA

Heavyweight Contest

DOUG   COVERMAN SPENCER

JOYCE   v   CHURCHILL

RUSHDEN T.V. Personality   KEW. Former Mr. Universe

Welterweight Contest
Black v White

LINDE   LEON

CAULDER   v   FORTUNA

WEST INDIES   FRIENDLY ISLES

Classic Welterweight Contest

DICK   ARCHER

CONLON   v   O'BRIEN

LONDON   CHELMSFORD

Luxury Seating At All Prices   ALL RIGHTS OF ADMISSION STRICTLY RESERVED

Prices 10/6 : 8/6 : 6/6 : 4/6 : 3/-

Advance Booking: **TED HARDY TRAVEL AGENCY**
24b Milford Street, Salisbury.   Tel. 2670

CAR PARK CASTLE STREET   LICENCED BAR APPLIED FOR

Ken often appeared on the bill fighting solo or in action alongside Eddie Capelli in matches with the European tag champions, the French Teddy Boys.

Ken Joyce.

A considerable number of wrestlers passed through the Hall in the Sixties. I will go into the wrestling in more detail in a later chapter, but a few of the Sixties bouts and characters are well worth a mention.

Salisbury wrestling fans were immensely privileged to witness a mysterious French heavyweight in action who went by the glorious name of Le Bourreau de Béthune (the Executioner of Béthune) – a name lifted from Alexander Dumas's 'The Three Musketeers'. With his purple garb and jangling cuffs, this enigmatic Frenchman cut a fearsome and bloodthirsty sight as he grappled his way unbeaten through his tours. Roy Bull Davis was a frequent victim. The Executioner has, in wrestling circles, remained a slightly romantic figure. It is known that he wrestled in his native France and also in Germany where he was known as Der Henker (the Hangman).

In 1966, the Zebra Kid wrestled Peter Fanene Maivia at the City Hall, or to give him his correct title, High Chief Peter Maivia. Peter was an American Samoan wrestler who came from a long Samoan wrestling dynasty. Also known as the Flying Hawaiian, he was easily identified by his tribal tattoos, which covered his abdomen and legs (apparently a symbol of his High Chief status). These had been applied with traditional Samoan instrumentation - a small hammer, a needle, and ink. His good humour, colourful trunks and an all-action style made him an immediate hit with the local fans. Many will remember Maivia lying across the top corner ropes for his inter-round relaxation! When grappling his opponents, he would counter any hold with a huge smile that would instantly remind fans why they loved him so much.

High Chief Peter Maivia.

High Chief Maivia hit the big time in 1967 when he appeared in the James Bond film, 'You Only Live Twice'. Shortly thereafter, he left Europe to concentrate on the promotional side of wrestling. Younger wrestling fans will however be more familiar with his famous Grandson, wrestler-turned-actor, Dwayne 'the Rock' Johnson.

Like High Chief Maivia, Zebra Kid missed out on the glory days of British wrestling, leaving the ring in 1968, so any wrestling fan that caught a bout between Peter Maivia and Zebra Kid was extremely fortunate. Zebra Kid was a mountainous twenty-four stone super-heavyweight, a fearsome sight in his striped mask. For a man of his girth, he was remarkably agile and skilful, even having a hand in training British Olympic wrestler Dennis McNamara. Born in the United States with Greek parents, Zebra Kid came to Britain in November 1959 and became a formidable foe in the ring. However, by the end of his wrestling career, he suffered a string of losses and un-maskings which ultimately led to his retirement.

Zebra Kid – masked!

The Wildman of Borneo also wrestled there that year. This extraordinary character had more than a passing resemblance to Cousin It from the Addams Family! Though billed at 18½ stones, this barefooted giant probably struggled in reality to reach the lower mid-heavyweight limit. He was for some reason used sparingly by promoters, so to see him on the bill at the City Hall was a treat. Clad in fur anklets and a leopard skin cape, he was a sight to behold and managed, in spite of the limited exposure, to become a household name. Mike Weeks (a City Hall Duty Manager) remembers the Wildman's hair used to fall in the face of his opponents causing some disorientation and annoyance!

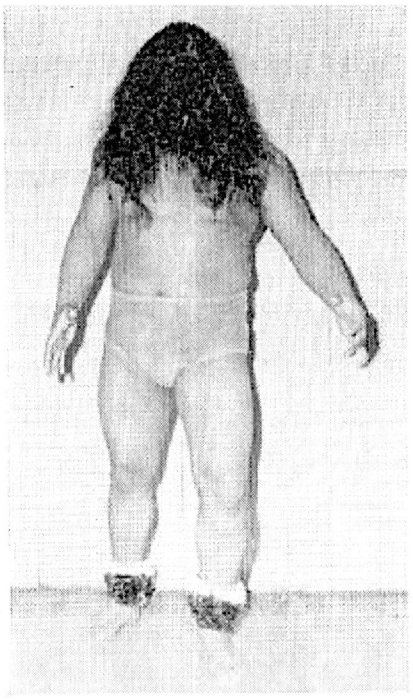

Bad hair day – the Wild Man of Borneo!

And finally (for now), Ken Joyce. Ken was British-born and Canadian bred. He turned professional in 1941 in Belfast against a South African wrestler called Ronnie Hurst. In those early days, he was known in some halls as 'Spindle' Joyce because of his slight physique. He was a well decorated wrestler who was a British and European welterweight champion. He also claimed the European tag-team championship with Eddie Capelli, though he also tagged with brother Doug Joyce.

Dances

The new City Hall also became the perfect venue for the local gala balls and dances, with its tiered seating, large open floor, large stage and ample foyer area. The Round Table used the venue regularly for its fund raisers along with the Motor and Allied Trades Benevolent Fund (as they are now known) who hosted their annual BEN Balls at the venue. The local Police Dances were also popular and often featured top big bands.

These events were always quite an occasion on the local calendar and were very well attended. The group picture over the page (by John Blasiak) was taken at one of the famous BEN Balls (1963 or 1964) and features from left to right, Wendy Catlin, Ken Lailey, Gordon Plum and Sally Plumb (nee Warner). Ken went on to make his name in special effects and formed the first ever local blues band. Gordon went on to manage local menswear store, Chas H. Baker.

THE SIXTIES POP DANCES

"Just absolute heaven – the best thing you could think of in the world."

Andy Nicklen describing the visiting Rolling Stones.

The Sixties were a truly golden age for the City Hall. As we have already seen, the venue had quickly become established as the local home of wrestling; S.A.O.S battled valiantly to stage their extravagant and popular shows and regular fundraisers were staged on a frequent basis for good causes.

However, in the eyes of the younger population, the real star of the Sixties was the seemingly endless succession of beat dances held throughout the decade, which drew in terrific crowds and the biggest names in pop and rock. Between 1963 and 1968, the City Hall was the mecca for popular entertainment in the area, beyond challenge and without rival.

In many respects, it was a lottery as to who was performing during a particular week. For instance, an evening of entertainment by such luminaries as the Gonks, the Meddy Evils or the Mob could be quickly followed by Manfred Mann, the Kinks or the Small Faces.

Whilst Saturdays were the big night for youngsters to blow their pounds, shillings and pence, it was common for dances to be held during week days as well.

So who else came to the Hall during this glittering era?

The very first big name in popular music to grace the City Hall stage was Craig Douglas, who had scored a major hit with 'Only Sixteen'. Returning to the Hall thirty-five years later as part of a tour package, he ruefully shared a story with the audience:

"I was recently approached by a fan who had named her son after me...he turned forty last week..."

A visit from the Barron Knights was followed in June 1963 by arguably the greatest band of all time – none other than the Beatles!

It was to be the Beatles one and only concert at the City Hall and had been booked in April by their manager, Brian Epstein.

The show was promoted by Jaybee Clubs, for whom the Beatles had performed in Stroud in March 1962. A fee of £300.00 was agreed but Epstein grew concerned for the safety of the band as their fame began to substantially outgrow the capacity of the City Hall and he offered to refund two thirds of the fee if the show was cancelled. It was to the benefit of the young population of Salisbury that Epstein's offer was declined and the show went ahead.

One thousand five hundred people turned up for the performance, queuing from 3p.m that afternoon. It broke all Salisbury attendance records for a one-off show and generated phenomenal memories for a whole generation, although artistically, the performance was unmemorable, in part because the girls were screaming so loudly and the Beatles' amplifiers were so tiny. It was very hard to hear anything.

Arguably, this performance opened the floodgates for other major bands to come to Salisbury. The City Hall, despite being open for just a few months, was well and truly on the map!

Autographs collected by Christine Gilbert, the Manager's daughter, during the Beatles visit.

Second only to the Beatles were the Rolling Stones. The Stones made a number of visits to the City Hall and despite having only a few minor hits at this stage, brought in crowds that could easily rival the Beatles. During one show, the police lost control of the crowd who ripped the curtain off its runners. It is difficult to explain why they attracted crowds of 2,000 plus when they lacked commercial success, but their tough image and long hair made them appear dangerous to teenagers – the very antithesis of the Beatles. Andy Nicklen, in an interview for the book 'Bend It' by Frogg Moody and Richard Nash described the gig as "*totally electric*" and "*just absolute heaven – the best thing you could think of in the world.*"

The Kinks appearance in April 1965 brought mayhem to the City Hall as the nice young ladies of Salisbury turned ferrell, storming the stage and putting the unsuspecting (and no doubt bewildered) stewards through forty minutes of sheer hell as the stage was rushed – all keen to have a piece of their idols. One girl, having allegedly collapsed, made a miraculous recovery on stage and grappled drummer Mick Avory to the ground. The curtain was eventually brought down so that order could be restored. Comparative calm followed and the show commenced without further interruption.

Andover boys the Troggs, appearing in their trademark pyjama suits, were subjected to similar treatment and lead singer Reg Presley was pulled off the stage and into the crowd! Not bad for a man who was carrying bricks on a building site just a few years earlier. Sadly, we lost Reg in February 2013.

In November 1966, the much anticipated Small Faces turned in a derisory performance – no more than ten minutes according to accounts. Front man Steve Marriott was not on his best form. Armed with a whiskey bottle in hand, he continued until his amp packed in and then headed off to the Fisherton Arms!

The psychedelic/progressive revolution was brought to Salisbury (via a fish and chip supper at the Yorkshire Fisheries) by Cream. The three-piece (Jack Bruce, Ginger Baker and Eric Clapton) were constantly clashing at this stage of their career. This incendiary cocktail graced the City Hall stage and performed to a static and unresponsive audience. At the end of the gig, Baker kicked over his drum kit, Clapton dropped and smashed a decent guitar and Bruce ripped the strings off his guitar by hand (not to be tried without thick gloves!) Baker was apparently very stoned, borne out in his own autobiography.

Another psychedelic band to play the City Hall during this era was a relatively unknown but highly creative group called the Pink Floyd, fronted by Syd Barrett. Few people cared for their visit and only a few dozen attended the gig. They showed slides during their performance and had a basic light show with various gels. Their set featured 'Arnold Layne' and 'See Emily Play'.

As much as Salisbury could (and still can) react positively to visiting acts, it can also be the master of apathy!

The City Hall also served as a great stage and spring board for many local acts, including Dave Dee & The Bostons. A re-shuffle in the line-up and a brand change to Dave Dee, Dozy, Beaky, Mick and Tich saw the group achieve huge fame with hits such as 'Bend It', 'Zabadak', 'The Legend of Xanadu' and 'The Wreck of the Antoinette'. It is possible that they visited and re-visited the City Hall more times than any other act between the Sixties and the publication of this book. In 2008, Salisbury Civic Society marked the success of our wonderful local heroes by erecting a plaque on the City Hall in recognition of their outstanding contribution to popular music and celebrating the 40th anniversary of their chart-topping single, 'The Legend of Xanadu'.

Sadly, in 2009, we lost Dave Dee to cancer.

Current manager Phill Smith pictured with the plaque

Who else played at the City Hall during this golden era?

Hold tight…here goes!

- Jess Conrad (who returned in the Nineties);
- Gene Vincent;
- The Swinging Blue Jeans;
- The Searchers;
- Freddie and the Dreamers;
- Johnny Kidd and the Pirates;
- Manfred Mann (see contract over page) who returned countless times as the Manfreds;
- Tony Meehan;
- Screaming Lord Sutch;
- Marty Wilde and the Wildcats;
- Brian Poole and the Tremeloes;
- The Hollies (who returned countless times);
- The Pretty Things;
- The Yardbirds;
- The Fairies;
- The Animals;
- Them;
- Lulu and the Luvvers;
- Georgie Fame and the Blue Flames;
- Chris Farlowe and the Thunderbirds (Chris returned with the Manreds almost 40 years later);
- The Move;
- Adge Cutler and the Wurzels;
- The Artwoods;
- The Herd;
- The Bee Gees;
- The Jeff Beck Group;
- Traffic.

This list is not exhaustive and many of the groups such as the Pretty Things returned many times over during the decade.

Contract signed by Paul Jones for Manfred Mann to appear at the City Hall

In 1968, the Alex Rooms opened in New Street, offering the City Hall its first real challenge as a venue for popular music. The number of gigs started slowing up and by the end of the decade, bookings of popular bands at the City Hall were virtually non-existent.

It was clear that times were changing…

(Over page: Salisbury's golden boys – Dave Dee, Dozy, Beaky, Mick & Tich on stage at the City Hall).

THE SEVENTIES

"Had it not been for the City Hall I would never have seen some of my greatest heroes."

Richard Coombs,
Salisbury photographer.

The Sixties had been a euphoric time for anyone growing up in Salisbury. The previous chapter is testament to that!

As a new decade approached, the City Hall's star was beginning to fade, with the nearby Alex Rooms in New Street picking up a host of popular acts for its regular Saturday night Alex Disco. Entertainment included Chicken Shack and Savoy Brown (both regulars visitors), Steamhammer, Manfred Mann, Juicy Lucy, Yes, Caravan, Procol Harum, Black Sabbath, Uriah Heep, Elkie Brooks, Gentle Giant, Thin Lizzy, Stackridge, Slade and Lindisfarne to name but a few…and that was just within the first two years.

Yet, during this same period, the City Hall could only attract a small handful of musical bookings, which included Mick Abraham's Band (ex-Jethro Tull) and Caravan. In 1971, after a particularly fallow period, the City Hall stage was graced by a 'double header' of Van Der Graaf Generator and a fledgling band by the name of Genesis.

The great Rory Gallagher also played the City Hall in 1971, but this could only be considered a warm-up to the final act of the year…the fortunes of the Hall were about to change, at least momentarily.

On 21st December 1971, the status of the venue was raised to a stratospheric level when it hosted arguably the greatest rock band on earth…the mighty Led Zeppelin!

This glorious treat for the youngsters of Salisbury was laid on by local entrepreneur, Peter Coombs:

"I organised this gig for the band. It was probably the smallest venue on the tour [Led Zeppelin had already played the United Kingdom, The United States, Canada and Japan in 1971]. *In spite of that, Peter Grant* [Manager] *and Mickey Most* [record label owner] *said it was 'a goer' and plans were made. Richard Cole invited me to the Wembley show early on in the tour so I knew what a treat was in store for the Salisbury fans. Jimmy* [Page] *was ill and the gig had to be postponed from the 15th until the 21st December. Support was by Martin James's band, Marble Orchard and Bob Cooke's Band (Ian Gillan's protégés,) Jerusalem. This was the most exciting concert Salisbury had ever seen or heard."*

This last comment was probably true, though there were some Beatles fans who might have disagreed with this sentiment.

With a seasonal atmosphere in the air, fans crowded into the City Hall. Mike Doherty recalls the venue being jam-packed:

"This gig was dangerously overcrowded. The demand for tickets was so high that more people got in than should have done. They started with 'Immigrant Song' and it was the loudest most impacting start to a gig I have ever seen. The crowd visibly moved back a few inches from the force of the sound waves."

Led Zeppelin played an awesome set which included 'Immigrant Song', 'Heartbreaker', 'Black Dog', 'Since I've Been Loving You', 'Going to California', 'That's the Way', 'Tangerine', 'Dazed and Confused', 'Stairway to Heaven', 'What Is and What Should Never Be' and 'Whole Lotta Love'.

The band could be heard all the way down Fisherton Street and it is fair to say that the building had not shaken so much since the air raid on 11th August 1942!

Ian Hussey remembers the gig with great affection:

This was the first rock concert I had been to. I 'blagged' a ticket off my mate Mick because his girlfriend could not go. It was a seminal moment of my life. I had not taken any notice of my mates raving about this group. I was 'skint' but went out next day and bought all four albums. It completely changed my view of how music can change the way you feel or think. Still the best live music I have ever, ever heard."

Following the gig, the band and their entourage retired to the nearby Provencal restaurant for a meal. A very fortunate City Hall Steward by the name of Tim Simons (who had missed his bus home) was apparently offered a lift to Bemerton Heath by drummer John Bonham in his Rolls Royce Convertible, capping one of the most extraordinary events to ever grace the stage of the City Hall.

Whether it was as a consequence of Led Zeppelin's headlining appearance or by pure co-incidence, the City Hall once again started seeing a more steady flow of regular contemporary music acts, including Free, Status Quo, Wishbone Ash, Welsh rockers Man (Richard Coombs testifies to falling asleep during this performance, he deemed it to be so dull) Uriah Heep, Desmond Dekker, Love Affair, Swinging Blue Jeans, Edison Lighthouse, Atomic Rooster (featuring Chris Farlowe) and West Country favourites Stackridge.

Salisbury also got a taste of glam rock with a hugely camp new band by the name of Roxy Music. The Bay City Rollers also performed at the City Hall, as well as massive stars of the time including Gary Glitter and Sweet. However, the biggest glam star of them all descended upon the venue one Thursday night in June 1973 – David Bowie!

The timing of the visit for Bowie fans was in hindsight incredibly significant, because it was less than three weeks before the fateful gig at Hammersmith Odeon when he famously broke up the band (captured for posterity on film and CD).

By the time Bowie and his Spiders had reached the City Hall, they were close to exhaustion. In those days, tours were lengthy and relentless, with few rest days factored into a tour itinerary. In fact, Bowie and his band had been on the road for twenty-nine days, often playing two gigs a day, with only one or two days off to recover.

Band members took the opportunity to have a look around the City prior to the gig. Richard Coombs takes up the story:

"My cousin Paul worked for Austin Reed gents outfitters at the time, in the Old George Mall. As we were assembling to go to the Bowie gig, Paul was telling us about this bloke with unfeasibly huge sideburns that had come into the shop earlier in the day. It wasn't until Trevor Bolder [Bowie's bassist] *came on stage that Paul realised who it was."*

A thousand people turned up at the City Hall for the show, having queued since six o'clock for the pleasure of seeing the greatest rock star of their generation.

They seemingly waited an eternity with repeated calls of 'we want David' falling on deaf ears. Then as the lights were dimmed, Bowie's sidekick and lead guitarist, Mick Ronson took to the stage, followed by Trevor Bolder and Mick 'Woody' Woodmansey (drums). Finally, Bowie leapt onto the stage and the City Hall exploded into life, bathed in strobe lighting, music and an electric atmosphere!

The concert was extraordinary, with Bowie getting carried along with the euphoria of the evening, at one point stage-diving into the excited audience, who thankfully caught him!

At one point, Bowie did his customary climb of the speaker stacks, leaping to the stage, but on this occasion landing awkwardly and hurting his ankle. Retiring from the stage for a period, he returned to complete the encore ('Round and Round') from a chair, telling the audience: *"I think I've broken my ankle. Not really, but it hurts a lot."*

As the show drew to a close, Bowie stepped up to the microphone to address his fans, telling them they were great and how they reminded him of the very first enthusiastic crowds that greeted them when they set off on tour a year ago.

Andy Golden of the Salisbury Journal captured the moment perfectly describing the concert as *"one of those never-to-be-forgotten moments which spans a lifetime but, in reality, lasts for about an hour."*

The set list for the show is not known for certain, but at around this time a Bowie concert typically comprised of the following:

'Hang On To Yourself', 'Ziggy Stardust', 'Watch That Man', 'Wild Eyed Boy From Freecloud', 'All The Young Dudes', 'Oh You Pretty Things', 'Moonage Daydream', 'Changes', 'Space Oddity', 'My Death', 'Cracked Actor', 'Time', 'Width Of A Circle', 'Let's Spend The Night Together', 'Suffragette City', 'White Light White Heat', 'Rock 'n' Roll Suicide', 'Round And Round'.

According to Frogg Moody and Richard Nash's book, 'Endless Beat', part of the show was later released as a bootleg LP under the name 'Quaaludes and Red Wine'.

The following day, Bowie travelled west to the Odeon at Taunton to play two shows. He was seen by a doctor as his ankle was still hurting but contrary to medical advice, he declined an x-ray and carried on with the shows. He performed most of the performances seated, being carried off at the end.

Salisbury clearly had enjoyed the best of him!

Another act that appeared in 1973 was German experimental progressive rock act, Tangerine Dream. 'Endless Beat' includes an enlightening interview with Salisbury Journal photographer Roger Elliott who photographed them on stage at the City Hall:

"I started at the Journal in September 1973. Prior to that time, apart from Dave Dee and occasional visiting celebrities, the music scene really didn't get photographed at all. Andy Golden used to review gigs and various reporters had taken an interest, but nobody had taken any pictures of all the bands visiting Salisbury in the Sixties and Seventies. I thought, 'well, I might as well start putting matters right'. The first one was Tangerine Dream – my first foray into the world of rock photography. They performed under very low light and after a while I thought 'what the hell am I going to do here? I'll have to use flash.' So I took the photograph with direct flash. The music stopped and I was admonished in German from the stage, so realised at that point it was not a good idea to fire flashes off in semi-darkness at professional musicians!"

Roger has consequently left music fans with a large and wonderful legacy and many of the images included in this book are down to Roger and his tenacity and dedication for being in the right place at the right time. Salisbury owes him a huge debt of gratitude.

As the decade progressed, the number of bands attending the Hall began to dwindle further. Certainly, there was the hugely popular Leo Sayer, who was the hottest act around at the time. He would have been promoting material from his 'Silverbird' and 'Just a Boy' albums. His set would have included 'The Show Must Go On', 'Giving It All Away', 'Long Tall Glasses' and 'One Man Band'. Leo was invariably accompanied at his shows by his Managers, David Courtney (who discovered him) and Adam Faith.

Barclay James Harvest and Arthur Lee's Love also played the Hall, but for the latter half of the decade, it was a sorry story which echoed the general state of affairs at the City Hall, which I shall explore in more depth in a later chapter.

The last few years were uncomfortably sparse for Salisbury in general, with the closure of the Alex Rooms. However, there was a rare and wonderful experience when Swindon's XTC played the City Hall (this band stopped touring a short time after this date due to lead singer Andy Partridge's stage fright).

And finally, the Seventies were aptly brought to a close on 21st December 1979 with our very own Dozy, Beaky, Mick and Tich.

Musically, it had been an interesting decade for Salisbury, even if it had been sparse. Richard Coombs, who spent much of the Seventies watching some of the biggest bands at the Hall, sums up this era very succinctly, perhaps speaking for a generation:

"I have very fond memories of Salisbury City Hall and the bands that played there in the Seventies. Had it not been for the City Hall I would never have seen some of my greatest heroes. As a teenager, it was a great thrill to be able to go and see the personalities featured in the likes of Melody Maker and New Musical Express. It was one thing to save up the money to buy the latest Wishbone Ash LP, but to see them play on stage was magical in every sense of the word. Things were different then. Those people were not as accessible as they are now with the internet. And for a couple of quid for a ticket from Ted Hardy's travel agents, it was a cheap night out, even then."

WRESTLING IN THE SEVENTIES

"The referee was running after the wrestlers shouting 'come back come back'".

Mike Weeks - MC and Time Keeper (pictured below in 2012).

I have touched upon the wrestling in the Sixties at the City Hall, but the venue really came into its own in the Seventies, regularly hosting matches between the top wrestlers in the Country.

Devereux Promotions was still firmly at the helm of wrestling at the City Hall and through their connection with Joint Promotions, they were guaranteed to secure the biggest names in the business. Joint Promotions was a nationwide group of promoters who worked co-operatively by carving the towns and cities of Britain into distinct territories and employing wrestlers under exclusive contract.

For the majority of the six hundred plus patrons who attended the City Hall every fortnight for their 'fix' of wrestling, they were going along to watch their heroes, their very own 'rock stars' who had graced their televisions screens on a Saturday afternoon, grunting and groaning each other into submission.

The more practical side of hosting wrestling at the Hall was less glamorous. Once a fortnight, Mike Weeks and Ken Harris would dig out the wrestling ring which was permanently stored at the Hall and set it up in time for the evening's entertainment.

On many occasions, Mike would act as time keeper, ringing the bell and keeping tabs on the rounds. Another role was to give out public warnings. Those of you that remember watching World of Sport or were actually at the City Hall wrestling matches in the Seventies, will recall that any wrestler deemed to be breaking the rules or who was generally misbehaving would be issued with a 'public warning'. Mike's job was to announce the warning over the microphone, reprimanding the offender. Mike loved this role and misses it very much. There was however one wrestler who was on the receiving end of Mike's reprimands more than any other, as he recalls:

"The worst offender was without doubt Mal Sanders."

Mal Sanders

Sanders was a superstar in wrestling terms and was a favourite with the ladies (who could resist the blond hair and yellow trunks?)

In the early days of his career, Sanders was a good, clean fighter but he soon started picking up bad habits from the likes of Syd Cooper and Zoltan Boscik, both regular bad boys of the ring.

Consequently, Mal ended up on the wrong end of Mike's wagging finger on many occasions.

The Devereux staff were asked to undertake all sorts of tasks but perhaps the oddest role of all time has to go to Ken Harris. During one particularly boisterous bout, one corner of the ring collapsed. This sort of thing rarely ever happened, but Ken was quickly to the rescue! Seizing the initiative, he stood in the corner of the ring and held up the ropes, acting as a human corner post, allowing the evening's entertainment to finish without any further hitches. He lived to tell the tale!

Other challenging issues included the task of actually getting the wrestlers into the ring. Giant Haystacks was 6 ft 11 inches tall and weighed in at somewhere in the region of 35 stone (this went up to 40-45 stone in the Eighties). The normal way for a wrestler to clamber into the ring was on one of the City Hall's grey plastic seats. Haystacks managed to buckle six of them under his weight one night as he tried to take his place inside the ring. The bill was sent by the Council to Devereux Promotions and from henceforth, the towering wrestler had his own special box especially constructed for this purpose.

One night at the City Hall, Mike Week's was in attendance as time keeper, watching the referee (Peter Jay) to see if any warnings needed to be issued. It was a good old family occasion for Mike as his wife, mother and brother Tony were all in attendance, watching avidly from the front row.

It was a particularly lively session as tag matches normally are. Steve Grey, very much the good guy, was on one team and Jon Cortez (always ripe for a few boos) was on the other.

Cortez and Grey were in the ring and Cortez very much had the upper hand. The audience was getting very agitated but it was all good fun. Then to Mike's surprise, his brother Tony had taken it upon himself to intervene! Tony climbed into the ring and grabbed Cortez, trying to pull him off his opponent, but unsurprisingly with little success.

To this day, Mike cannot properly explain why he did what he did next, but he climbed into the ring and leapt onto Jon Cortez's back!

Cortez was far from amused, snarling at Mike *"I'll kill you, you b...!"*

Well, the audience loved all of this and went completely wild, cheering for 'the Weeks brothers!' They were not advertised on the billboards but they were damn good entertainment!

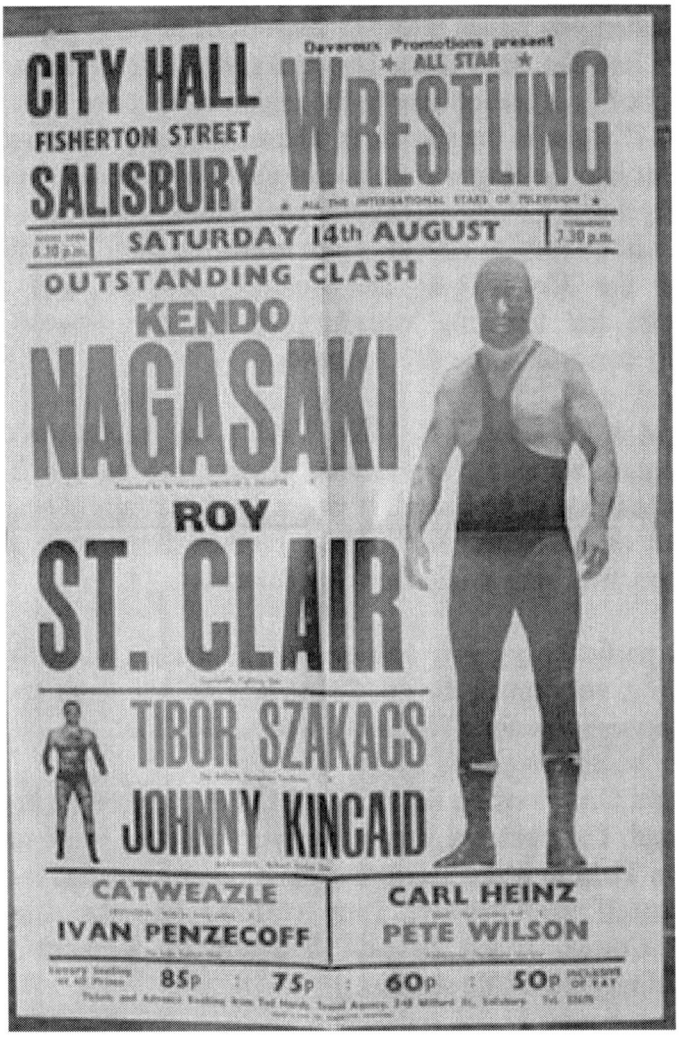

But Cortez had not finished with Mike and he was not going to let him off lightly. Grabbing his 'new' opponent, the helpless timekeeper was tossed into the air, landing on the canvas in an undignified heap, before crawling out of the ring.

The only damage Mike sustained was a bruised pride and a couple of broken ribs. Ken Joyce of Devereux Promotions was so impressed that he gave him a pay rise!

In the late Nineties, I was fortunate enough to enjoy an evening of wrestling at the City Hall. The names on the bill featured some of the heroes from the golden age of wrestling including bad boy Mick McManus and wrestler-turned-actor, 'Bomber' Pat Roach (pictured).

Pat Roach

Pat spared some time for an interview with me behind the curtains on the main stage. A towering, bearded figure, he was a gentleman in every sense. He had started his wrestling days as 'Big' Pat Roach but had adopted the name 'Bomber' after playing bricklayer Brian 'Bomber' Busbridge in 'Auf Wiedersehen, Pet'. And just like Sixties wrestler Peter Maivia (featured earlier), he went on to carve out a second career in film, also appearing in a Bond film, in Pat's case the Connery revival, 'Never Say Never Again'. He also featured in 'A Clockwork Orange' and the Indiana Jones films.

Pat was often cast in the role of the bad guy along with McManus, but his endearing personality and high profile saw this all change, and he was taken to the heart of the fans. On one occasion, he was wrestling at the City Hall, when things got terribly out of hand, as he explained to me:

"Much of the audience at the City Hall comprised the local gypsies and travellers. It had become known that I was descended from 'water gypsies', so they were firmly on my side. During one match, I was taking quite a beating and the crowd got so annoyed, they chased my opponent out of the Hall and down Fisherton Street!"

Pat had to try and calm the situation down and rescue his hapless opponent who was at risk from a serious beating!

Mike Weeks remembers the evening well:

"The referee was running after the wrestlers shouting 'come back come back'".

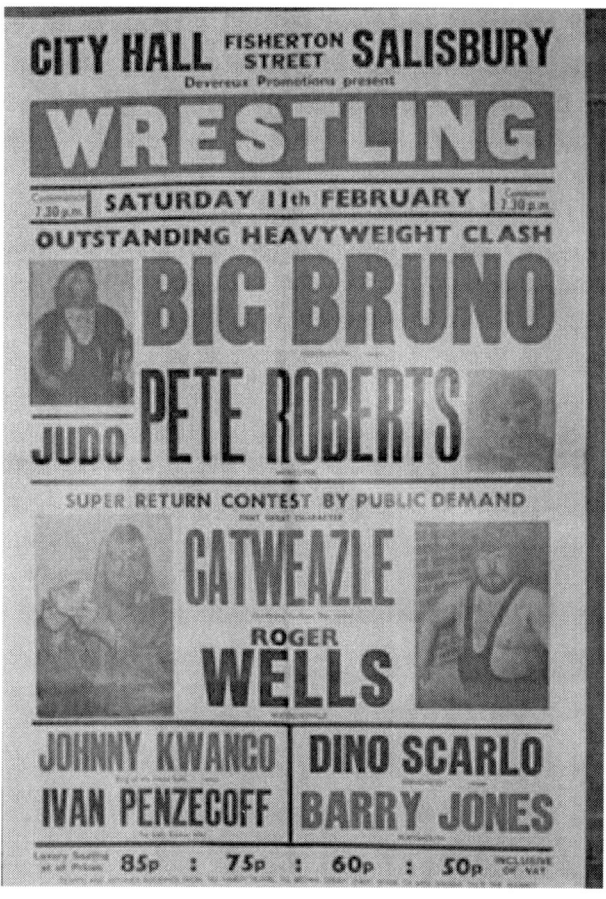

You will see from some of the posters included in this book that there were often 'race' tag bouts – black wrestlers versus white wrestlers. I put it to Mike Weeks that these may have been racially motivated, but he was quick to strongly disagree:

"On the contrary, nine times out of ten the audience was behind the black guys."

Of the visiting wrestlers during this wonderful era, a few are worth a special mention for old times' sake before closing this chapter:

In 1975, Mike Marino fought the great Judo Al Hayes at the City Hall. Marino was a classy wrestler and a personal favourite of Mike Weeks. Marino's opponent was making one of a few appearances on his last wrestling tour of the United Kingdom. 'Judo' was regarded by colleagues as a wrestlers' wrestler, a marvellous tactician and a joker in the dressing room. He was also popular outside the ring. In 1968, he became a Conservative councillor in the Labour stronghold of Islington. He was also a keen historian, and a golfer. Shortly after leaving the ring at the City Hall, he went off to America and fought 'American Style' wrestling as 'The White Angel'. He retired in 1995.

The scowling and hardened features of Hungarian born Zoltan Boscik made him a wrestler that fans found easy to dislike. He was a skilled wrestler who usually stayed just on the right side of the rules, but he fitted the part of the 'baddy' through and through. He was a true 'grappler' and relentlessly applied punishing holds, making him an entertaining figure in the ring.

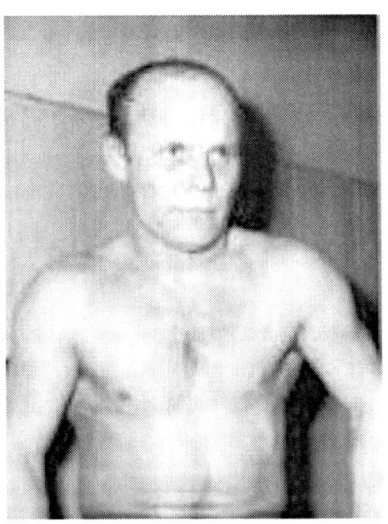

Zoltan Boscik.

Johnny Kincaid became one of the country's top wrestlers who could compete with the best in the business, including Mick McManus. Kincaid became a complex fighter who was both loved and loathed by the fans. He had started his career from the bottom up, competing in the fairground wrestling booths, before getting his big break in the late Sixties.

Dave 'Butcher' Bond was an imposing figure who frequently grappled and grunted his way to disqualification, no doubt earning public warnings from Mike or Ken Harris. He was a master at stirring up the crowds and getting their backs up. His rugged features made him an inevitable villain, which he played to perfection.

Polish wrestler Johnny Czeslaw (pictured below) was a regular at the City Hall and was hugely popular with the fans. He had a reputation for resuscitating the dullest of wrestling matches. He was an occasional tag partner of Ivan Penzecoff and amused the audiences with the odd shout of "*Schwein!*" when getting to grips with an opponent. Unlike many of his opponents, he could often be found watching the wrestling, which he genuinely seemed to enjoy.

Another wrestler who could often be found in the audience at Salisbury was the mysterious Mr X. It seemed that no one knew his real name (not even Mike or Ken) and he would watch avidly, waiting for something untoward to happen in the ring, at which point he would jump up and challenge the offending wrestler. This would then set him up for a bout the following fortnight, when his name would be splashed over the local posters and flyers.

One of the most famous and enigmatic heavyweights of the ring was the mysterious Kendo Nagasaki. Nagasaki wore a red and white striped mask for the majority of his career and claimed to be permanently undefeated, although he was often disqualified. He was often accompanied by his flamboyant manager, 'Gorgeous George' who would take to the ring before Nagasaki to fire up the crowds. The wrestling bouts were not allowed to begin until certain ceremonies had been completed, including the throwing of salt around the ring (a process meant to cleanse any post-fight ill will). Kendo Nagasaki was technically superb and at times relentlessly brutal. He was finally unmasked in 1977, but he has always remained a curious and somewhat mysterious figure.

The enormous Giant Haystacks has already featured in this chapter, working his way through the City Hall's seating. He was a huge draw at the Hall. When (eventually) making it into the ring, he would often lean over the top rope to abuse the crowd. The poor chap who happened to be in the ring with him was often despatched to the canvas with the greatest of ease, struggling to cope with the surprisingly nimble giant. Haystacks was privately a deeply spiritual man with strong business acumen.

The fans' favourite was the one and only Big Daddy. With his glittering cape, top hat and union flag jacket, he was an unmistakeable figure. He would stand in the middle of the ring clapping along as his fans chanted "easy, easy." His 'Big Daddy Splash' often brought the desired knockout against his more slim line opponents and tears to the eyes of the audience! It was often imitated by youngsters in the playground, including the author!

In truth, whatever anyone felt or thought about the wrestling, it helped to keep the City Hall afloat, or at the very least, keep the financial deficit down and also ensured that whatever else was going on at the time, six hundred plus people religiously processed in and out of the Fisherton Street entrance every fortnight for an evening of uninhibited laughter and entertainment. After all, wasn't that what it was all about?

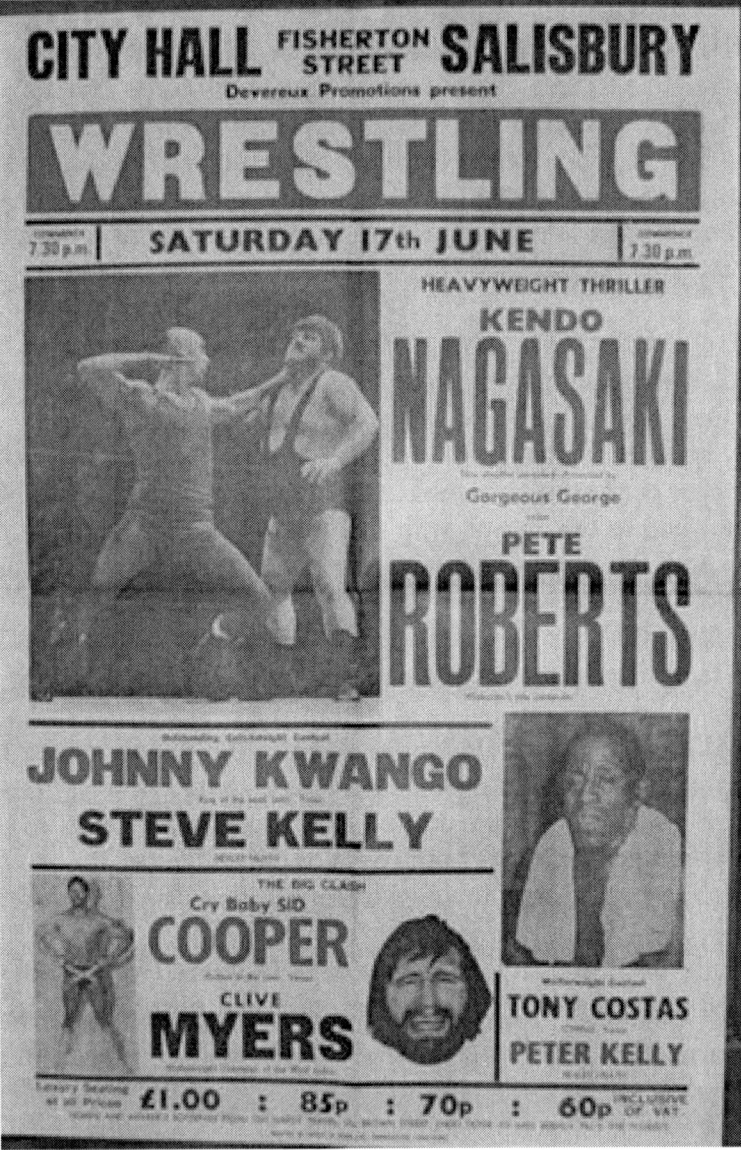

AMATEUR IN NAME ONLY

"Being another character is more interesting than being yourself."

John Gielgud

Throughout the previous chapters, we have touched upon some of the more entertaining and successful aspects of the history of the City Hall, including Salisbury Amateur Operatic Society, an organisation that pre-dated the Hall by some fifty-plus years.

The Society was founded on 23rd July 1908 by a small band of gentlemen who thought they could culturally enrich the local population with their amateur operatic productions. Gilbert and Sullivan productions were a favourite and consequently, they launched themselves on the population of Salisbury with the 'Pirates of Penzance', which has become a firm favourite with the Society down the generations. For this first production, police uniforms were borrowed from the local constabulary!

Lord Radnor graciously agreed to be their President and he was in turn followed by his son, the Earl of Radnor. To my knowledge, the Society is only on its third President in one hundred plus years, the Honourable Mary Morrison D.C.V.O.

Early performances were staged at the County Hall in Endless Street which became known as the Palace Theatre. In 1912, proceeds from a show were given to local relatives of the brave orchestra which went down with the Titanic.

For a time after the First World War, the Society located to the Victoria Hall in Rollestone Street (now home to the Salisbury Journal). The building was in fact the local baths which had a floor added so that it served a dual purpose. However, they returned to their home in Endless Street before re-locating to the old Picture House in Fisherton Street.

Here they stayed until the City Hall was opened in 1963.

Joyce Bowden, now Vice-President of the Society, joined in the late Forties.

"In those days, the leading men tended to be older gentlemen – it was quite an elderly Society"

However, members of the Society were not above a practical joke as Joyce elaborates:

"During one production, I was in the lead role and one of the stage hands tied a kipper to my dress, which everyone could smell on stage!"

By the time the Society had moved to the City Hall, a younger generation had started to come on board, offering a vast array of talent and skills.

Productions staged at the City Hall during the Seventies and Eighties included such favourites as H.M.S. Pinafore, Kiss Me Kate, My Fair Lady, Fiddler on the Roof and the Mikado (a full list can be found at the back of this book).

Leading lights within the Society during this period included Trevor Locke and John Pinder who helped to ensure that the highest standards were maintained.

Viva Mexico - 1974

Die Fledermaus (1978) (Trevor Locke & John Pinder)

Guys and Dolls (1987) (John Pinder and Nigel Swatridge)

Here are a few highlights from the era:

The Merry Widow - The Merry Widow was a bold and lavish production to stage and had never been performed at the City Hall until now. It was a strong production, though Salisbury Journal noted that it was at times over-crowded and over-fussy. Joyce Bowden was excellent in the lead role of the merry widow, playing opposite John Pinder as Count Danilo. The show pulled in a staggering four thousand two hundred people over six nights; just six hundred light of a complete sell-out. This could be regarded as an absolute triumph for a provincial amateur group.

Hello Dolly - This Spring production undoubtedly belonged to Betty Huish who was appearing in her fiftieth production (which she also claimed would be her last). Betty took the leading role as Dolly, playing opposite the dependable John Pinder as Horace Vandergelder. This was also noteworthy for being Ray Jeffrey's fifth production with S.A.O.S.

The Gypsy Baron (1982)

Iolanthe (1981)

Hello Dolly (1977)

The Land of Smiles (1983) (David Coxon and Beverley Cutler)

Trial by Jury & The Pirates of Penzance - Trial By Jury is a one act play by Gilbert and Sullivan. It was often staged as part of a double or treble bill by the professional companies but as a stand-alone production by amateur groups, so for S.A.O.S to stage it as a forerunner to another challenging production was brave indeed. And they managed to pull off both Comic Opera's in style! Trevor Locke bravely took lead roles in both productions but arguably the star performance was that of John Pinder in The Pirates of Penzance.

By the end of the decade, it was felt that the Society's presence should be marked at the City Hall. Accordingly, a new commemorative cabinet was installed. The cabinet, located in the foyer, sought to mark the history and longevity of the Society and was 'opened' by the Chairman of Salisbury District Council, John Abbott, in the presence of senior members of S.A.O.S.

South Pacific (1986) (Jim Dolman and Peter Watts)

The 'opening' of the cabinet (L to R): Jack Roberts, Alfred Wallbridge, Joyce Bowden, John Abbot, Edward Woodward, Arthur Bennett, Betty Bowden, Francis Pullen, Bill Bowden

WHITE ELEPHANT?

"It reminds me of a village hall committee like we used to have after the war."

Councillor Hedley Farris.

From reading the earlier chapters in this book, you can see that the City Hall had become a valuable community asset. However, by the mid-Seventies it was in dire trouble.

An unexpected guest at a charity event

In 1975, Salisbury District Council's Recreation and Amenities Committee (affirmed by the Council's Finance Committee) significantly ramped up the rates of hire for both the City Hall and the Guildhall. The cost of booking the main auditorium at the

City Hall for an average night almost doubled. The Council's Assistant Financial Controller, Brian Coveney explained to the Recreation and Amenities Committee that another £2,500.00 was required from the City Hall to keep it in line with 1975/76 financial estimates.

Unfortunately, the result of this rash decision by Council Members had a catastrophic effect and backfired in spectacular style.

By January of 1976, one of the Hall's biggest promoters had pulled out. Giles Larner had regularly booked the Hall for his disco nights which had proven to be immensely popular. A normal booking fee of £39.00 was payable to the Council for the privilege, but this had now leapt to £69.00 making the continued use of the Hall untenable. Mr Larner had passed on the cost to the youngsters attending the discos by upping the ticket prices but the net result was that attendance figures dropped from an average of a thousand a night to about three hundred and fifty.

The consequential loss of revenue to the Council for the year was £2,000.00…not far off what they had tried to make back by pushing up the hire rates in the first place.

In fact, Mr Larner went on to hire St. Michael's Community Centre at Bemerton Heath for £18.00 per night – a lot less glamorous but far more practical from a business viewpoint.

A mystery promoter offered to take over the discos for a trial period when youngsters complained about the move to Bemerton Heath, offering some light relief to the City Hall's financial crisis.

The Council was not only feeling the consequential effects of the price rise but the effect of a lack of promotion too. During the Sixties and early Seventies, the Hall had pretty much bank rolled and promoted itself. It was new, everyone was aware of it and it was on the main concert/dance circuit, meaning that virtually every self-respecting band and artist that toured the country, ensured that the City Hall was on its itinerary.

Mr Larner's news only added to a worsening situation. The Christmas of 1975 had already been bereft, with no major peak time bookings at the Hall (bar S.A.O.S and one or two other regular events) and the diary for 1976 was looking decidedly empty too.

Despite the bad news, Des Lumley, the Council's Finance Committee Chairman and Dickie Lodge, Chairman of the Recreation and Amenities Committee, backed the City Hall, but a view was emerging from certain quarters of the local community that the building was no more than a white elephant.

Lodge reluctantly admitted at the time:

"If we closed the City Hall we would be better off...but I think we have got to have the City Hall."

As the year progressed, the Hall's problems became more acute. Its annual income of £8,000.00 per annum was no match for the running costs of £30,000.00, with the Council's Financial Controller, Cyril Rowe, ramping up the pressure on the Recreation and Amenities Committee to take some form of action:

"The income in relation to the expenditure is ludicrous and the expenditure is increasing all the time. If conditions were worse, you might seriously have to consider closing this hall. Public halls in general are a loss."

Another option considered was the abolition of the one third discount given to charitable, cultural and educational bookings. These amounted to about half of the total bookings received by the Hall, but also reflected the nature of the Hall's use by the local community. The suggestion drew outrage from Gil Burden who addressed the Council's Finance Committee:

"I am disgusted at the thought of abolishing the one thirty three and one third per cent discount for charitable, educational and cultural bookings. This would penalise the very type of person who gave so much towards the hall when it was built after the 1939-45 War" [not factually accurate as the Hall was built in 1937]. *"Just after the War a Victory Hall fund was set up and subscribed to by a number of charitable organisations within the City. In recognition of what the city charities and organisations had done towards raising the capital, it was granted that they should have a one third reduction on bookings. The Hall is a memorial to those people who gave their lives during the 1939-45 war, and when we start thinking that this thing should raise a profit or pay for itself I get annoyed."*

Bill Lambert added his support to Gil Burden's comments:

"If you deny them the use of the Hall, your losses are going to be very much greater."

Thankfully, this idea was dropped. At the time of going to print, the Hall still offers a discount for such bookings, which currently stands at twenty per cent.

Another option put forward was the possible closure of the Hall on Sundays to avoid paying double time wages to staff, on the basis that any mess created on a Saturday night function could be cleaned up on the following Monday.

These were desperate times indeed and Alderman Moore's words must have been echoing in their ears:

"The ultimate success of the hall will be gauged rather by the extent of its use than by its income and expenditure account."

It was one thing to lose money, but with the building being grossly under-utilised, the Hall was rapidly becoming a failure on all fronts, which must have been a travesty to those who campaigned for the building in the first place and contributed generously to the Memorial Fund.

By August 1976, there seemed to be an alternative option emerging which for some councillors was extremely appealing but for others, was too much to stomach.

A West Country entrepreneur by the name of Michael O'Grady came forward with an offer to lease the hall and turn its £22,000.00 annual loss into a comfortable profit. O'Grady had a proven track record for taking over similar stricken venues and had scored successes in Yeovil and Bridgwater, pulling in between three and four hundred people a night for a multitude of different events. He now had the City Hall in his sights:

"I have been trying to find a place in Salisbury for some time," he told Jo Silcox of Salisbury Journal. *"I'll be prepared to turn that loss of theirs into the same amount of profit if they allow me to lease it. I realise that city people are loath to relinquish their hall to an outside organisation, but they are not professionals. Any hall run by the ratepayers has a certain kind of 'squareness' about it, which can lead to financial troubles like yours. It needs someone running it who has a personal vested interest in it…I would love to have that place. I know I could make it come alive again."*

O'Grady was right – the Hall did indeed have a certain 'squareness' about it. The building was not particularly warm or welcoming (a far cry from the days of The New Picture House), its promotion was almost non-existent, patrons had no idea how to hire the Hall due to the lack of signage and in any event, the cost was probably beyond the pockets of many individuals and organisations. It also needed approximately £80,000.00 spent on it to bring it up to date; the last refurbishment took place in 1963 and the building was in need of some serious attention.

And finally, it did not appear to have a manager in charge – Len Adams had long since retired. It all seemed inconceivable by modern standards.

Michael O'Grady invited members of the Recreation and Amenities Committee to visit his other premises, an offer they chose to accept, but the ensuing debate that followed clearly ruffled feathers.

Anthony Stocken (a Councillor and well-known local architect) was adamant that if an outsider could make the Hall work, then he was sure the Council could do the same. Prophetically, he was correct, but it would take many years for his optimism to be borne out. It was clear that despite their best intentions, the current regime did not have the capability to make a proper go of things.

One of O'Grady's suggestions was to extend and sound proof the Alamein Room increasing its functionality and earning potential, a suggestion which caused frustration to Stocken as he had suggested the very same thing himself at an earlier date.

Other members of the Recreation and Amenities Committee were keen to take up the external offer. Both Hugh Aubrey and Dorothy Gray wanted the Hall to be farmed out for the good of the City and its citizens. Too much money had been wasted.

Perhaps Hedley Farris came closest to the root of the problem:

"It reminds me of a village hall committee like we used to have after the war."

No doubt with heavy hearts but with a firm eye on the future of the Hall, members of the Committee voted by nine votes to six to endorse (in principle) the City Hall Sub Committee's decision to place the venue into private hands, possibly on a twenty-one year lease.

By 1977, nothing further had happened. The Council had chosen not to take up Michael O'Grady's offer but to go it alone with a new plan of action, in the hope that they could change the fortunes of the City Hall.

One of the decisions was to appoint a full time Manager. Supporting the new Manager would be a full-time Clerical

Assistant, a full time Attendant and a team of cleaners who would also clean the Guildhall.

The Council also resolved to spend £6,300.00 on both structural repairs and promotional improvements to the Hall and a further £2,500.00 was committed to converting office accommodation. However, Councillors were finding it hard to justify spending any more money when the projected losses for March 1978 were estimated to be £25,000.00.

Indeed, by 1979, the same old problems persisted with a projected expenditure of £67,400 in return for an income of just £14,500.

So what was the REAL problem that blighted the Hall during the Seventies?

Well, it certainly hosted some high profile events that brought in large crowds, but these were too few and far between. The majority of the major events booked in by promoters attracted the normal booking fee, so the Hall was not sharing in the tickets receipts, which is often where events really made money (although there was also the risk of sharing in the losses too if an event failed to sell).

It also had too few regular major bookings. The wrestling was a staple diet for the Hall and S.A.O.S brought in large crowds, but this was based upon two productions per year. Indeed, during the Seventies, the Society was extremely worried that they were going to be made homeless with all the threats of closure.

And finally, these were hard economic times. Inflation was high and generally, people did not have a lot of money to spare.

However, the Hall had somehow managed to survive a tumultuous decade and whilst not being in proper shape to take on the Eighties, was at least still functioning, despite having its fair share of critics who (to some extent quite understandably) viewed it as a money pit.

Perhaps the saddest or most undignified blow of all was to the beautiful façade of the building. In what many may consider a callous act of vandalism, the front, left hand wing of the entrance was torn down to make way for Summerlock Approach, leaving the frontage looking odd and imbalanced.

RE-MAKE RE-MODEL

"[The entrance] was far better in Fisherton Street. People think the place has closed down."

Pip Brown – local trader.

As the Seventies gave way to the Eighties, there seemed little respite for the City Hall as it continued to turn in a succession of poor financial performances, leading to continued heavy losses.

In 1984, Salisbury District Council took a momentous decision. Previous efforts at throwing small, unplanned amounts of money at the Hall had proven to be pointless. It was therefore decided that the Hall needed a massive overhaul.

This was not to be a minor undertaking. The idea was to create a building that was more versatile and adaptable than the current design, enabling it to cater for conferences, banquets, dances, concerts, exhibitions, stage shows and indoor sports. The thinking behind the makeover was to enable the venue to take more than one booking in an evening, allowing different events to run side by side. It was also hoped that success would have a knock-on effect within the City, attracting a new hotel and perhaps other businesses besides.

The main auditorium was to feature a six thousand square foot sprung maple floor. It would also have full stage facilities (no doubt to the delight of S.A.O.S) which would include thirty six lighting channels and eight sound channels as well as a selection of backdrops and comprehensive scenery options.

New floor and tiered seating

It was also planned that the auditorium would have flexible seating arrangements for 1,250 people. This ambition did not however come to fruition, with seating being restricted to 953 people, or a total of 1,116 standing (this gives you some idea how overcrowded some of the dances were in the Sixties!) It could also accommodate 800 at a dance and just over 500 at a dining event such as an awards evening.

The new foyer

Perhaps the most innovative idea behind the revamp was the new bank of foldaway seating to be installed at the back of the hall, which could seat 495 people over fifteen rows. This could be electronically wheeled out or folded away within a matter of minutes. It was an inspired purchase.

The auditorium would also be supported by a brand new set of spacious dressing rooms with mirrors and shower facilities.

The building would have a separate meeting room above the original entrance and the Alamein Suite was to be upgraded and sound proofed to allow for competing events. It was to benefit from sliding partitions and a separate entrance.

The plans were both brave and innovative, creating a fabulous 'new' venue for Salisbury, but it had its dissenters. Independent Councillor Tom Cowie described the scheme as *"dealing with a white elephant by giving it an expensive coat of whitewash."* He had also described it as *"ill-judged, ill-advised and incredibly stupid."*

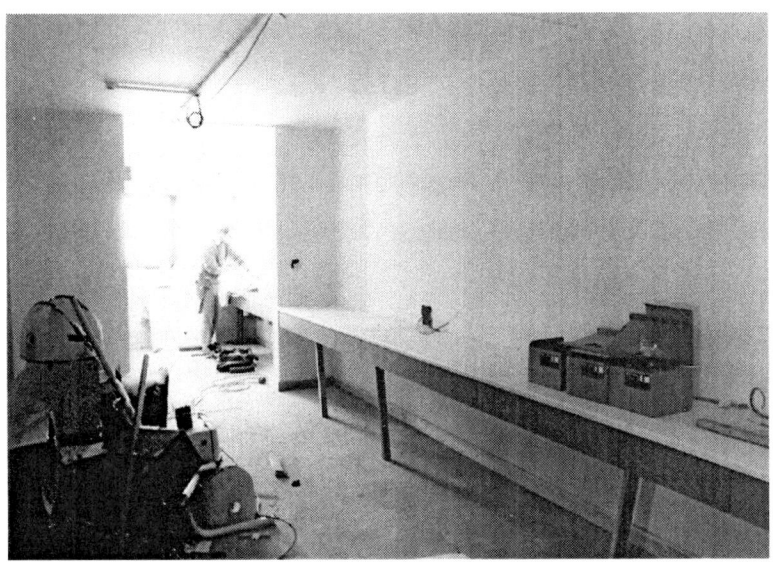

Brand new dressing rooms

Council Chairman John Burden also had concerns, worried that the Hall would fail to attract bookings in the number anticipated to make the project a success. In truth, these concerns were probably shared by the majority of the Council Members and senior staff, but a feeling of optimism permeated and drove the project forward.

At the end of 1984, the building shut up shop for a year. The Whicheloe Macfarlane Partnership designed the changes to the building and the building work was undertaken by John Laing Construction.

It was a phenomenal undertaking and the pictures featured in this book give you some idea of the scale of the job.

Laing's had their fair share of problems with the construction work. Hiding beneath parts of the City and in particular the Maltings, is liquid chalk. As they drilled into the ground, it poured out of the holes and froze on the surface like pink coral, giving head Architect David Radford some major headaches! Laings drilled fifteen metres into the soft chalk, embedding twenty-metre piles in the underlying clay. It was effectively like trying to pump concrete through porridge.

Another issue was the maize of old drains running under the venue, most of which were still in use. Whenever Laing's stumbled across a drain, they had to change their plans and consult with the Architects; no doubt a total nightmare for the Quantity Surveyor whose job it was to keep a lid on the cost elements.

Throughout the building works, there were two highly controversial changes. The first was the removal of the main staircase which was a design feature, and the second was the abandonment of the classic 1930s entrance. Whilst the inclusion of the new entrance adjacent to the Salisbury Playhouse made a certain amount of sense, it robbed the building of its true character. The original Trent-designed frontage, once proud with its neon signs, canopy and flagpoles, was now a sorry shadow of its former glory, looking forlorn alongside the Fisherton Street shops. It was architecturally nothing short of a catastrophe.

Roger Godwin, proprietor of the Shoe & Leather business opposite the old City Hall entrance was soon to discover the pitfalls of this move:

"When the front was eventually blocked off, I was forever getting people in the shop asking how to get to the Hall. It was quite embarrassing to have to tell them that they had to traverse a grotty little alleyway to find the new front entrance on the side."

New entrance under construction

Pip Brown of Stonehenge Cycles of Fisherton Street had similar feelings about the closure of the original entrance.

"It was far better in Fisherton Street. People think the place has closed down."

Internally, many of the art deco fixtures and fittings had either been destroyed or masked, in many respects changing the look and feel of the building for all time.

The controversial new entrance under construction.

The spacious new loading bay.

But setting aside these (albeit significant) issues, the conversion was a success and arguably secured the future of the Hall, which had lived under a cloud for so very long.

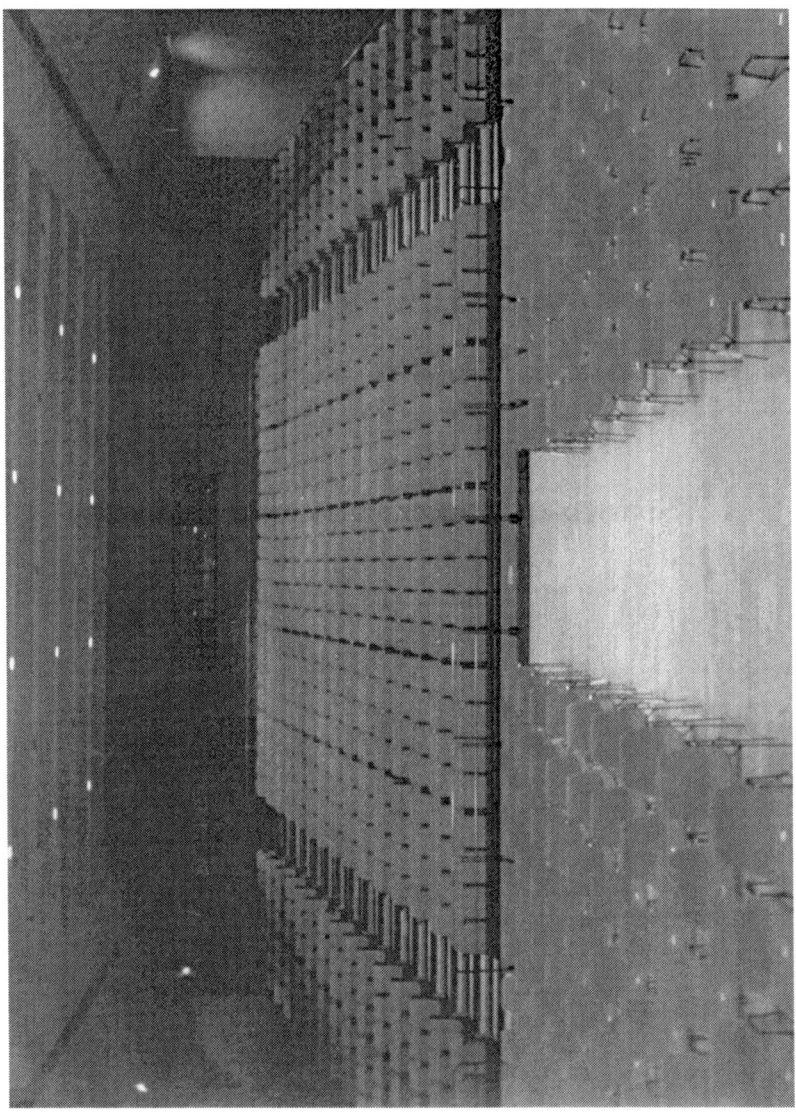

By the end of 1985, the works had been completed. Attending the handing over ceremony was an optimistic Councillor Burden and the conversion's greatest critic, Tom Cowie, who ironically happened to be in his Mayoral year. The photograph of him that appeared in the press during the handing over ceremony showed him putting on a brave face as he performed his Civic duties, but clearly it did not sit comfortably. Others present at the ceremony included Frank McLoughlin, Director of John Laing and Laing's Regional Director, Peter Rowe.

The total price paid for the entire work was £848,000, a phenomenal sum in the Mid-Eighties but the amount of work achieved for this price was considerable. The keys were handed on to the Manager, Jack Wills, who confirmed that during the refurbishment process, there had been plenty of enquiries. There was also a leafleting campaign under way promoting the virtues of the newly converted building as one of the most adaptable venues in the South.

Two open days were held on the 17th and 20th December 1985, allowing the public to view the new works. On the 17th, the Hall was re-dedicated as a war memorial by The Bishop of Salisbury, the Right Rev. John Baker, who also re-dedicated the memorial tablet which can be found in the foyer. It reads:

'As a lasting tribute to the Citizens of Salisbury who served in the Second World War 1939 – 1945, the provision of this Hall was made possible by the united efforts of our community.

The Hall was opened on the 30th January, 1963, by Alderman Francis J, Moore, Chairman of the Salisbury Victory Fund Committee, and this plaque was dedicated by the Lord Bishop of Sherborne, the Right Reverand V.J. Pike. C.B., C.B.E., D.D., (Suffragan Bishop of Salisbury).

Councillor S.A. Vokes

Mayor.'

The City Hall re-opened for business on 3rd January 1986, beckoning in a new era for the building since its last conversion in 1963.

Amazingly, this was the first time it actually sold its own tickets. Members of the public always had to go to Ted Hardy's travel agency to buy tickets for any event, but this was at long last localised, giving the Hall greater control over ticket sales. The days of running the venue like a village hall were fast becoming a distant memory.

The first major event staged at the revamped Hall was a GALA Charity Ball held by the Salisbury Rotary Club, with entertainment provided by The Syd Lawrence Orchestra and the Real Ale And Thunder Band.

The first gig to be held was Fairport Convention, who are now old favourites at the venue. They came close to being the first sell-out event of the new era.

Fairport Convention

The honour for the first new production surprisingly did not go to S.A.O.S, but to Godolphin, Warminster and Bishop Wordsworth Schools for their joint production of Gilbert and Sullivan's Mikado on the 9th - 11th January 1986.

And there was a splash of culture to the new surroundings when the newly formed Sarum Chamber Orchestra took to the stage on 1st February, conducted by Howard Moody (then a mere twenty years of age). The Orchestra featured talented local musicians including Daphne Handford (violin) and Michael Stubbs (viola). The programme included pieces by Bach and Mozart.

Devereux Productions soon returned with their wrestling shows. They still attracted a fair crowd, but the lack of television exposure meant that the average attendance size had now begun to fall away. Many wrestling fans felt that the sport had become stale and failed to move with the times.

It is fair to say that following the revamp, the Hall was coming in for regular use, particularly from local schools and charity groups such as the Lions and Rotary Club for their dances, but it failed to attract too many high profile names...the type of names that ensured that the Hall was making money and regularly full to capacity. And whilst there had been some successes, there had also been quite possibly the greatest marketing disaster in the history of the City Hall when the legendary Detroit Emeralds sold just nineteen tickets. Both band and fans could have comfortably fitted into the new meeting room upstairs without any need for taking the main auditorium!

But there was now a serious problem which had become very noticeable. On the occasions there had been a full house, the temperature in the auditorium had become unbearably hot.

When the Council was planning the budget for the refurbishment, a number of items were sliced from the 'to do' list to keep the costs down. One such item of expenditure was the air conditioning unit. Unfortunately, the existing unit was simply not capable of bringing the temperature in the Hall down to a comfortable level. The experience was particularly bad at the back of the tiered seating.

The Council realised their error in cutting this item and committed a further £40,000 in order to rectify the problem. Tom Cowie, perhaps the most vocal objector to the Hall's upgrade was far from impressed:

"Every means was used to push this project forward to its disastrous end!"

Councillor David Parker, a vocal supporter of the City Hall for many years, felt that the overall result of the refit could have been so much better:

"For nearly a million pounds, we deserved a whole lot better."

Hindsight and history are a wonderful thing to have on your side, which these Members did not have at the time. However, by taking the bold step to spend the money and upgrade the City Hall, they were safeguarding its long term future by putting the building blocks in place for some very successful years to come.

Unfortunately, the short term view was not looking good.

From talking to people who worked at the Hall during this post-refurbishment period, it is clear that Jack Wills and his Assistant Manager Doug Goodman gave the re-launched City Hall their very best effort. They brought people in through the door for a vast array of events and applying Alderman Francis Moore's original rule of thumb, their tenure could be regarded as a success – the Hall was busy!

Events included an array of regular discos, the Salisbury Police Ball and other dances, amateur boxing, fortnightly wrestling as well as acts such as Lindisfarne, Peter Skellern and Lenny Henry and of course S.A.O.S. No one could accuse Jack Wills, Doug Goodman and their team of not trying…

However, applying the hard facts of modern economics, the building was once again in financial trouble and was causing some serious concern; and given the major investment, maybe it was time for a change.

As one former colleague from this era commented, *"things just seemed to stall."*

Pictured – a South Wilts Grammar School prom

PHOENIX

"Perhaps [the City Hall] doesn't do anything absolutely perfectly but it does a lot of things only marginally imperfectly."

David Rawlinson

Chief Executive, Salisbury District Council.

The late David Rawlinson

In February 1989, the history of the City Hall took a dramatic twist, taking the building off in a whole new direction.

The City Hall had failed to achieve its full potential for the best part of two and a half decades and it seemed that the glamour of the cinema days and the swinging Sixties were a distant memory.

However, the Council decided to make a bold new appointment in the hope of ushering in a new era. She was the Hall's first female Manager and her name was Barbara Softley (pictured).

So, where did Barbara come from and what gave her the qualification to run a struggling entertainment venue?

Well, Barbara had a proven track record as a firm but fair manager, albeit at a different type of facility - Durrington Pool. Prior to this she had been involved in the closure of Salisbury's outdoor pool and had played a significant role in opening Salisbury's new replacement indoor pool at the top end of the City.

So whilst she certainly had never run another theatre, she had proven herself as a very capable and well liked manager.

When Barbara took over the City Hall it really did look like her appointment was 'the last throw of the dice'. So, with a feeling of some trepidation, a pay rise and a new six month contract (with the promise of her old job back!), Barbara set up office in what she describes as *"a rather smelly"* City Hall.

Barbara's appointment was not without some contention. She faced a certain amount of opposition from certain councillors and senior managers which made her job very difficult, but Chief Executive David Rawlinson and Councillor Eileen Casley threw their support behind her and in effect, gave Barbara the mandate she required to get on and turn the Hall around. Another great supporter was Councillor Olwyn Tanner, who has always been a keen ally of the venue.

One of Barbara's first challenges was to build up the mailing list. This was a matter of great foresight because building up a database is key to getting people to buy tickets. From then on, it would be possible for Barbara to target her audiences. A classic example was a busy weekend during Barbara's tenure, when Stilgoe & Skellern played on a Friday, followed by Jethro on the Saturday. Other than the stewards on duty, it is highly unlikely that any one fee paying member of the audience attended both nights. The former brought in the city folk and the sophisticates. The latter brought in the farm hands and country folk. And to Barbara's credit, both nights sold out, and much of this was down to the power of effective marketing and her ability to target her audiences.

In no time at all the mailing list had increased from 2,500 names to a staggering 18,000; roughly one in five of the population of Salisbury District (as it was then).

She also introduced a brand new computerised ticketing system, bringing the venue kicking and screaming into the twentieth century. Barbara also turned her attention to the auditorium, overseeing improvements to the sound and lighting.

She also rebuilt her team from the ground up, as she explains:

"I hand-picked most of the staff at the City Hall, from the cleaners up to the management. We had the best team in Salisbury and we were all very hands on."

However, she also faced a far more difficult task – changing public perception of the City Hall. A decade and a half of troubles had left it firmly (and often unfairly) tagged a 'white elephant'. Salisbury Journal conducted a series of interviews with members of the public during one busy week in the Summer of 1989 and the enormity of Barbara's task soon became apparent. John Blackwell, Landlord of the Bird in Hand in North Street had a commonly shared view:

"It's not for the population of Salisbury. I travel to Southampton if there's a big do on."

Amanda Lisowski had a similar view:

"My husband and I like going to Bournemouth International Centre (B.I.C) to see cabarets. I haven't been to the City Hall for years. The last thing I went to see was a cookery demonstration but there weren't many people there."

Helen and Duncan Bendermacher said they liked the Sixties music but had not been to see any of the oldies revival concerts at the City Hall. They thought this might be down to a lack of advertising.

Her answer was to book Kylie or Bros. In fact, Amanda Lisowski had made a similar suggestion, encouraging bookings for Cliff Richard and Dire Straits!

And here lay the challenge that faced Barbara and her team. Salisbury City Hall could not realistically compete with the B.I.C, or for that matter, the Mayflower in Southampton. It would take some serious powers of persuasion to attract some of the bigger acts that were guaranteed to sell out the venue.

Barbara's tenure got off to shaky start with the ill-fated 'Ten Days In May'. A series of veteran music acts were booked back to back but many failed to draw in the crowds and the Hall lost many thousands of pounds as a consequence. Some of the choices were quite inspired. Lonnie Donegan went down well with the Salisbury faithful, as did Marty Wilde with the Swinging Blue Jeans and Kenny Ball and his Jazzmen. However, the booking of Mungo Jerry, the Equals, the Swingle Singers and Ed Bruce and his Tennessee Cowboys were all cancelled due to a lack of interest. And whilst some of the blame had to rest with the Council, often it was public apathy that saw events at the Hall fall flat.

Trevor Locke, a leading light with S.A.O.S, was at a loss to understand why the venue failed to pay. He had checked out the figures for the same period at Portsmouth Guildhall and it was consistently selling out events, whereas the City Hall had lost money on no less than fourteen consecutive promotions in the main auditorium.

Barbara's problems were further compounded when the sound proofing, installed before her tenure, failed to keep two conflicting events apart. It happened on a Saturday night when a packed auditorium was enjoying a concert by regular visitors, the Sarum Chamber Orchestra. However, those at the back of the tiered seating found the sound of a disco in the Alamein Room bleeding through into the main theatre.

Richard Seal, Salisbury Cathedral organist, was far from impressed:

"The sound proofing in that hall is notoriously bad. But on this occasion the noise from a disco in the Alamein Room was enough to ruin the entire concert."

Peter Grove, who attended the concert had this to say:

"Did the management seriously think that a thin wall would be adequate separation? Did it think at all when it made the simultaneous bookings? If such contempt is the way to keep the hall profitable, then let it close forthwith and stay at home or go to Poole for our classical music."

The latter statement was extremely harsh given the amount of money and effort that had been put into modernising the hall. It was true, the sound proofing fell short of what was required (it was not the thin wall alluded to by Mr Grove), but in truth, only the last few rows of the tiered seating had apparently been affected.

One of the intentions of the 1985 refit was to encourage the running of events side by side. This was in order to keep the flow of revenue coming into the building in view of its historical financial woes. However, it was accepted by Barbara and her team that, given the building's limitations, it would have to pick and choose which events were run in tandem. It was not 'contemptuous', it was simply unfortunate.

Councillor David Parker was quick to side with the new Manager:

"It seems the management can't win. We need much more use of all parts of the Hall. We cannot afford to turn away business if we are to please ratepayers and cut the subsidy on the Hall. Other 'clashing' events have been held there with little or no problem...the days have gone when one part of the Hall can be booked and the remainder left unused. Don't fire at the

management team while they have had their hands tied and their backs to the wall. The staff are doing a superb job."

Despite this shaky start, by the early Nineties, Barbara had taken a firm grip on the venue and was pulling off some startling successes.

One theme she had hit upon was the booking of male strippers. In 1991, she tentatively booked the Dreamboys and was staggered when nine hundred women hot footed it down to the Hall to catch a glimpse of toned male flesh!

At last, here was something that definitely stirred certain members of the local population! Members of the excited audience included veteran Councillors Eileen Casley and Pat Errington-Rycroft.

The event made a comfortable £2,000.00 and was soon followed throughout the decade by bookings and re-bookings of similar acts, including Adonis and the Chippendales.

The Chippendales used to cause a stir by sitting around the foyer area in the minimum of clothing – an absolute treat for the female members of staff but more than a little disconcerting for the male employees! The dance troupe generated scenes at the Hall not seen since the Sixties and Seventies, with hundreds of screaming women queuing outside waiting for the doors to open.

Such shrewd bookings had proven a turning point for the City Hall. By 1991, the financial fortunes of the Hall were looking up. Back in the Seventies, it was losing four times as much as it was earning. Now, it was managing to cover half of its running costs, a substantial achievement. Not only that, but 80,000 people came through the doors that year, the equivalent of four-fifths of the local population.

Throughout the decade, Barbara hit upon a winning formula.

West Country comedian Jethro was a sure-fire hit, coming back year after year and selling out on every occasion with his own special brand of comedy and plenty of tales about 'me and my mate Denzil.' Indeed, he was consistently the biggest booking of the Nineties.

Another regular booking was Danny La Rue. There is no question that Danny was the undisputed 'Queen of Drag', but he was also very high maintenance and staff would run for cover whenever he was booked in. However, he was immensely popular and pulled the crowds in every time.

Barbara Softley recalls an incident when Danny was in the building and the fire alarms went off. Barbara found Danny backstage standing in his corset. When she tried to usher him out of the building, she was told in no uncertain terms to "*fuck off!*"

When the City Hall reached its sixtieth anniversary, Danny kindly agreed to cut an anniversary cake on stage prior to the interval and posed for photographs with former Usherette, Beryl Robson.

During the Nineties, there was also a big trend for hypnotic acts, brought about by Paul McKenna's television shows. The City Hall capitalised on this by bringing hypnotic shows to the venue, which were well received and well attended, unless of course you spent the whole show in a trance which happened to more than one poor theatre goer. Adam Knight was a master of his art, hypnotising members of his audience into performing like Madonna, a Chippendale, naughty school children and Elvis!

Other visitors included Rik Mayall, Victoria Wood with her clever word-play, Lenny Henry, who would test out new material on the Salisbury faithful, Jasper Carrott and that fabulous all-round entertainer, Roy Castle. Norman Wisdom was a huge hit as well, amazing audiences with his antics, including falling off a piano, despite now being well into his Eighties. More risqué was Ruby Wax who was always on our television screens around this time.

Rik Mayall

All round entertainer Des O'Connor was a big draw as well as poet Pam Ayres. But perhaps one of the most prolific visitors (who at the time of going to print is still a regular at the City Hall) was Ken Dodd. Ken's shows would often be five or six hour marathons, only winding down after a member of staff (often Assistant Manager Graham Jackson) had wandered onto the stage and dropped the keys into his hands. Even now, Ken Dodd can fill City Hall almost to capacity.

Music fans were treated to an excellent mix of talent including local girl Toyah (on a number of occasions), Sister Sledge, the Blues Band, the Climax Blues Band, Hugh Cornwell of the Stranglers and Dr and the Medics as part of the Arts Festival.

Toyah

Clive 'the Doctor' from Doctor & The Medics

The visit of Canvey Island hell raisers, Dr Feelgood, threw up quite possibly the most outrageous tour rider that the City Hall had ever received from a visiting band. For the uninitiated, a tour rider is a list of back stage 'wishes' containing refreshments for a visiting act and their entourage. Salisbury's Essex visitors excelled themselves, with a list containing enough beer, lager and spirits to sink the Titanic! Needless to say, Barbara declined it.

'Medicinal purposes only' - The late, great Lee Brilleaux from Doctor Feelgood

For the 'folkies', there was Ralph McTell, The Fureys, Fairport Convention and the Dubliners. Although none of these acts could be deemed as 'current', they were popular and all helped to put the City Hall back on the map.

The Dubliners

For those that loved jazz, Kenny Ball and his Jazzmen pulled in a sizeable audience, only to be outsold by 'Georgeous George' Melly and Humphrey Lyttleton. Melly's visit with his 'Feetwarmers' was marked by his trademark red and cream pin stripe suit and a nerve-wracking 'wobble' when he stood on the edge of the stage to 'neck' a double whisky. The gasp from the audience was audible as he sank the beverage, then rocked gently back and forth until he regained his composure.

I have previously gone into some detail about the wrestling. Staggeringly, some of the big names from the golden era in the Seventies were still visiting the venue. These included Big Daddy, 'Bomber' Pat Roach and Mick McManus. However, the tide was clearly turning against British wrestling and American-style wrestling was becoming a staple diet for the youngsters who were now perhaps too young to remember the big stars of their parents' era. Audiences now averaged about three hundred, leaving the City Hall half empty, but still bringing in just enough people to make it all worth the effort.

Other sports included Amateur Boxing hosted by the Lions Club and a number of high profile snooker exhibition tournaments, featuring a very young Stephen Hendry, Steve Davis, Willie Thorne and John Virgo.

For lovers of ballet, The Vienna Festival Ballet visited on a number of occasions, adding a splash of culture to the programme of events. Sarum Chamber Orchestra, Soiree Musicale Ensemble and Bournemouth Sinfonietta also continued to be regular visitors.

For those that like a touch of brass, there was the Glenn Miller Orchestra, the Rhythm Aces, the Herb Miller Orchestra, the Band of the Grenadier Guards and H.M Band of the Royal Marines to name but a few.

And finally, there was S.A.O.S who continued to test the capabilities of the Hall and draw in tremendous crowds with their shows.

Here are a few of them to jog your memory:

Carousel was a monumental production. Not only was it a near sell-out, the revolving carousel set was greeted with a spontaneous round of applause from the audience. For a supposedly amateur production, the standard throughout was superb, with technically and artistically excellent performances. The choreography is worthy of a special mention (choreographed by Kim Yew Wong), making difficult and often complex dance routines look very easy.

The Yeoman of the Guard - It had been in 1975 when S.A.O.S last staged this Gilbert and Sullivan classic. As ever, the costumes and sets shone out, providing a visual feast for theatre goers. Lorraine Blakey was singled out for special mention for her role as Elsie. Stuart Gibbons brought the house down as the broken hearted Jester, Jack Point and the moving 'I have A Song To Sing O'.

Hans Anderson was all about the children. There were two teams of twelve local youngsters who appeared on different nights. Salisbury Journal described this production as 'a cracker of a show', which shone through with its lovely costumes and clever lighting. Barry McIlroy directed the production and Stuart Gibson starred as Hans.

Sweet Charity - S.A.O.S favourite Peta Seabright starred in this production, bringing warm-hearted charisma to the lead role. Again, the show was fabulously choreographed by Kim Yew Wong. Fran Vokes had her hands full directing this production given the large cast, but could be rightly proud of the end result.

Half a Sixpence was last staged at the City Hall in 1976 and was therefore long overdue for a revisit. On this occasion, Bryan Newman took Tommy Steele's role of Arthur Kipps and made it very much his own. He apparently shone, with his singing and dancing skills. As a show, it held together well, with the usual lovely costumes and excellent choreography.

Cabaret - the staging of Cabaret was a bold step away from the 'run-of-the-mill' Rodgers & Hammerstein and Gilbert & Sullivan productions. Set in pre-war Berlin, the cast delivered an intelligent and thought-provoking production, with notable performances from Sally Bowles and Christian Jull.

The Mikado - this was the third time Gilbert and Sullivan's The Mikado had been staged at the City Hall. David Turner produced a tight show which had all the classic S.A.O.S hallmarks, including great costumes, sets and singing.

Barnum - following the relatively 'safe' production of The Mikado, the staging of Barnum was arguably one of the most brave and challenging productions ever undertaken by an amateur company. Members of S.A.O.S spent months attending regular workshops to perfect their skills on the tightrope, trapeze, trampoline and unicycle in preparation for the show. Christian Jull starred as Barnum with Nikki Angel playing his wife. The results (which I can testify from seeing this first hand) were absolutely stunning!

Me And My Girl was last staged by S.A.O.S in 1961, so it was making its debut at the City Hall. Kevin Catchpole commented upon the production thus:

"Praise be for John Dempster's vibrant instrumental support and the magical works of London Stagesets, skilfully switched before our eyes by Colin Matthews and crew. The large company got a little tangled in enthusiasm and confined space along the opening road. But quick changes and lively routines eased the show along. The footwork, too, was a delight. [The] highlight was the brilliant Lambeth Walk, complete with pearly king and queen. But the real pearls were always Gay's tunes."

A Christmas Old Time Musical - Those of you old enough to remember 'The Good Old Days' on television in the Seventies, would have loved this nostalgic evening of 19th Century entertainment, chaired by popular local figure, Arthur George Bowden. The show featured some familiar local names, including Alison Babey, Lorraine Blakey and Nikki Angel-Jull.

Rhythms of Life – this ambitious show helped S.A.O.S close their first century in existence with a host of songs covering the previous one hundred years. Dee Adcock of Salisbury Journal noted that the songs seemed to improve as the century progressed. S.A.O.S included songs from the musicals Hair, Grease and Jesus Christ Superstar.

South Pacific - it had been thirteen years since the last production of this highly popular musical, so arguably it was due a revisit. Fans were treated to one of the most popular and well known soundtracks of all time including the wonderful 'Happy Talk', under the musical direction of John Dempster. Martyn Knight directed the production which starred Claire Sainsbury and David Coxon.

I have in some detail covered the exploits of S.A.O.S throughout this book and rightly so, as they have filled the City Hall consistently for over fifty years. But spare a thought for Salisbury Light Opera Society (S.L.O.S). This was a small but determined group of individuals steered by Beverley Cutler, who splintered off from S.A.O.S and staged their own shows. They were successful in raising funds for their own productions and worked extremely hard, but did not have history on their side and despite their best efforts, rarely came close to filling the City Hall. They no longer exist but they staged a number of shows during the Nineties at the Hall, including Hello Dolly.

This decade also saw the newly formed independent radio station, Spire FM, take up residence in the top rooms at the City Hall. They have been in residence for over twenty years; no mean feat for a small radio station during these difficult economic times.

By the time Barbara announced her retirement in 1997, bringing her eight years in charge to an end, it is fair to say that she and her dedicated team had turned the City Hall around and secured its future for another generation. It had not all been plain sailing, but the Hall was now 'fit-for-purpose' and ready for a new manager to take the helm and steer the venue into the 21st Century…but who would the Council choose?

INTO THE 21ST CENTURY

"It's a privilege to have a job in an area that I am so interested in – music and entertainment. I've also been very lucky to work with some very talented people."

Phill Smith (2013)

I mentioned in the previous chapter the success of the Guildhall in Southampton. Part of that success was down to their Operations Manager, Phill Smith.

Phill originated from Stoke, had cut his teeth in the entertainment industry as an assistant manager in a cinema. Relocating to the South coast, he enjoyed a fruitful spell in Southampton before being offered the role as Barbara's successor. Despite still only being in his thirties, he had enough experience under his belt to know how such a venue was run, which made him a logical choice for the position.

Phill knew that many of the acts booked by his predecessor had been a huge success, not least the likes of Jethro, who remained a regular booking. But he also took the City Hall down a more contemporary route.

His first ever booking was Peter Green (formerly of the original Fleetwood Mac) and his Splinter Group. It was not a sell-out, but it was popular and helped to act as a litmus test for future bookings.

He followed this with other contemporary acts including the Stranglers and bravely started pushing to secure the sort of entertainment that would quite easily have filled far bigger venues. A classic example of this was the booking of Supergrass, a band at the very peak of their fame who could easily have filled the Bournemouth International Centre. It was a huge coup and something Phill is no doubt very proud of.

Dee Adcock meets the new Mr City Hall

My hall's a stick of rock or soccer club

PHIL Smith is fond of analogy. It comes naturally to him to see Salisbury City Hall as a football team and as a stick of rock.

Actually, he has got a point.

As the hall's new manager, he sees the venue right at the top of division two. "We'll never be in the premier league — you've got to be realistic and accept that. But we're at the top of the second division ready for promotion into the first, it's perfectly feasible."

Making it happen is where the stick of rock comes in.

"I like to think that the City Hall's a stick of rock, the word quality right through it," he said.

"Wherever you cut it, you find the word quality. That applies to our customers whether they buy a ticket or hire the City Hall for a private event. It applies to everyone we deal with, including promoters and agents."

He is quick to point out that he took over an already successful venue when he was appointed manager in April.

Even so, changes are inevitable and some will gradually be seen as the Phil Smith touch filters through in new programming.

The new season reflects the blend. Regular favourites will continue, including the Chippendales, and the Christmas concert by the Royal Marines band.

But comedy, rock and blues bands, jazz and unusual events like the Gary Rhodes cooking roadshow are likely to become more typical of the venue's programmes.

"Children's shows, classical concerts and events from the local community have always been a strong point here," he said. "They sell well and are successful.

"But some areas are under-exploited. I'd like to develop the music programme in all areas from rock to jazz to classical and have more comedy.

"Trying to get the balance right is the biggest challenge. We are a receiving house so what we can put on depends on what there is.

"In the last couple of years, for example, there has been an explosion in the number of tribute bands.

"Top-nature bands, the huge names, like Oasis and Blur, appear at only a third of the venues they would once have had on a national tour. Salisbury simply doesn't get on the stopping list.

But Phil is keen to use his contacts from years of staging events at Southampton's Northguild complex to bag the mega bands on their way up.

It could take a couple of seasons to feel the extra strands in the programme but he is confident the City Hall is getting there.

"I've asked the staff to dig out the sold-out signs," he said. "We're going to need it."

Phil Smith: "We're ready for promotion to the first division but we'll never be in the premier league."

Staff picture

Phill's first booking – Peter Green

Supergrass

The musicians that followed read like a 'Who's Who' of music – Gary Numan, Fish from Marillion, Van Morrison (who usually played the Mayflower theatre in Southampton), Morrissey, N-Dubz (more familiar with the O2 Arena), Richard Thompson, Kate Rusby, June Tabor, Joan Baez, John Mayall, Chickenshack and the Oysterband. Regulars from Barbara Softley's era also returned, including Fairport Convention, who continued to draw in the faithful.

In the same way that his predecessor had tapped into the genre of the times, Phill followed suite, securing the services of various tribute acts, including the Australian Pink Floyd, the Illegal Eagles and Live Wire (AC/DC tribute), all of which proved to be immensely popular.

Phil also brought in fresh comic talent, some of which had performed at the O2 Arena in London, including such giants as Alan Carr and Peter Kay.

The wrestling also continued to be held at the City Hall, but not as often as in the previous three decades. All but a few of the big names of British wrestling had now retired, opening the way for a new generation of American-style wrestlers to compete against each other. Audience numbers however, had dwindled from six hundred plus in the Seventies, to three hundred plus in the Nineties, to less than two hundred a show, placing a question mark over the City Hall's future as a wrestling venue after half a century.

In 2008, S.A.O.S reached their one hundredth anniversary. They celebrated with a dinner at the Haunch of Venison, where the four founders of the Society first met. Current members felt that the founding fathers were there with them in spirit.

Here is a précis of some of the shows they staged during the first decade of the 21st Century:

The Pirates of Penzance was the very first production ever staged by S.A.O.S. This was the third time it had been staged at the City Hall and the ninth in total. The show was stunning, with amazing costumes and a wonderful set. Special mention must go to S.A.O.S veteran Lorraine Blakey for her portrayal of Mabel and Sue Crouch, who stole the show as Ruth.

Oliver! was the second S.A.O.S production of the millennium. This popular show pulled in large audiences and received rapturous applause, not least for the performances of Tommy Andrews as Oliver and Tom Woolford as the Artful Dodger. Geoff Heard policed the hordes of children as the incorrigible Fagin.

Guys And Dolls in 2001 took the Society in an altogether different direction. As usual, the costumes were fabulous but it was commented upon that the production lacked pace and atmosphere although the singing was, as ever, excellent. There were, however some excellent individual performances including Roger Ganner as Sky Masterson and Tina Lucy's Miss Adelaide.

The Wizard of Oz was the second show of 2001 and was a triumph! The City Hall stage was turned into a fantasy land dominated by strong colours and complemented by wonderful costumes. Director Barry McIlroy must take credit for putting on an amazing show which captivated its audience. Claire Sainsbury played Dorothy, with Vince Kemm stealing the show as the Scarecrow. Roger Ganner's Cowardly Lion also went down well with the audience.

The Merry Widow - after taking us to a land of make-believe the previous year, S.A.O.S contrasted this with a comfortable old operetta. This is not an easy production to perform and Lorraine Blakey and David Coxon were perfect choices in the lead roles. The Merry Widow was last performed by the Society at the City Hall in the mid-Seventies during a time of strikes and deep austerity measures.

Fiddler on the Roof - this was S.A.O.S's third production of 'Fiddler' since the City Hall opened. Last time around the lead roles were taken by John Pinder and Joyce Bowden. On this occasion Geoff Heard, Jill Cocovini and Dee Mansfield starred. Heard was excellent as Tevye and his efforts were appreciated by the audience.

Orpheus in the Underworld - Hot on the heels of one old classic was another, the ever popular 'Orpheus'. Dee Adcock commented thus:

"Show-goers wafted away to another world with this lavish production. It had all the comforts of waltzes and velvety costumes an air of nobility and a completely silly story. Company and audience simply fell into each other's arms in old-fashioned adoration of a fine old show, lovingly presented. Like true aristocrats this operetta is demanding and fastidious. Only the best singing, the choicest costumes, a top orchestra will do."

What high praise indeed!

Oklahoma! was the first show staged by S.A.O.S at the City Hall and it was time to dust it down and give it another outing in 2003. Barry McIlroy was at the helm as Director and put on a show full of vitality, though Kevin Catchpole commented that some of the dance routines appeared almost too challenging for the singers. He also commented that the stage struggled to cope with a fifty-strong company. Special mention must go to Julian Jeffrey as Ali Hakim and David Coxon as Jud Fry.

Scrooge - this was S.A.O.S's first attempt at this, which they achieved despite the fact that the facilities at the City Hall were not ideal for a show with difficult scenes and special effects. The singing and dancing were excellent throughout and the creation of a Dickensian England very compelling. Geoff Heard's performance as Ebenezer Scrooge was described as 'masterful'.

My Fair Lady was celebrating its fiftieth anniversary when S.A.O.S chose to re-stage it in 2006. This particular production was well sung and acted in front of some substantial audiences.

Nicky Burgess gave a stunning performance as Eliza Doolittle. Christian Jull is also worthy of a mention for his part as Henry Higgins. Once again, Geoff Heard also excelled. The musicians are often overlooked in theatre reviews. John Dempster and his orchestra complemented the production throughout

Iolanthe took S.A.O.S to new heights under the guidance and Directorship of Alistair Donkin, a former member of the D'oyly Carte Opera Company. The show was full of energy, enthusiasm and great costumes - a great way to cap their ninety-ninth year in existence. Special mention must go to Michael Bolton for his dedicated performance as the Lord Chancellor.

Titanic the Musical was first staged in 1997, so S.A.O.S were close behind with their own take on this great story. A show like this was never going to be easy to stage and on this occasion, the Society relied upon black drapes and projected slides of various locations. Alec Ruddick of the National Operatic & Dramatic Association felt this was somewhat dull. However, he felt that the uniforms and the props were in keeping with the period. All in all, not the easiest production to stage in a regional theatre. Financially, the show hit a metaphorical iceberg, losing a staggering £15,000, which resulted in a flurry of fund raising to keep the Society on an 'even keel'.

The Pirates of Penzance - in 2008, S.A.O.S went back to their roots for their centenary production with an old favourite, the Pirates of Penzance (in fact, the second production of 'Pirates' that decade). This was indeed the very first show they had staged, way back in 1908. The show lived up to their excellent reputation with great singing and wonderful costumes. The founders would have been proud, had they known that one hundred years on, their Society was still going strong and keeping the standards high!

The King and I – for the second centenary production, it was back to the ever popular Rodgers and Hammerstein. Martyn Davies took the lead role as the King with Claudia Shakerley as Anna. Malcolm Clarke took the Director's chair for the first time for the Society and had his hands full, with a host of musical numbers and thirty children to direct!

The Mikado - the last time this had been staged by S.A.O.S was in 1997. The show had pace, the lighting was excellent and the orchestra and singing were first class. It was a captivating production which drew the audience in at every level.

The Full Monty was another departure from the tried and tested formula of the 'oldies', bringing to life a production which attracted a predominantly female audience (perhaps suffering withdrawals from the days of the Chippendales at the City Hall!) Such was the expectation for a glimpse of local flesh that opening night numbers doubled to over six hundred! It was a nicely paced production, well-rehearsed and comically well timed. Special mention goes to Danny Simmons for his performance. The Salisbury Journal was however a little reserved in its praise of this production.

42nd Street – Kate Sibbald starred in her first S.A.O.S show and brought the house down with her portrayal of Peggy Sawyer. Indeed, this whole production was a major challenge for a provincial group, but the Society rose to the challenge and delivered a highly competent and well received performance in all respects.

The Gondoliers – it had been over thirty years since the Gondoliers had been staged by the Society. Alistair Donkin, a man well versed in Gilbert & Sullivan, directed the show and the results were pleasing, with good comic timing, lovely costumes and a generally slick production all round.

The Sound of Music – 2011 closed with S.A.O.S's daring production of the Sound of Music. In many respects, this is a musical that can sell itself, due to the vast array of well-known and much loved songs. Laura Kitching (otherwise known as 'miss' to the pupils of Downton Primary School) stole the show as Maria, supported by an immensely able cast including Michael Bolton as Max Detweiler, Helen Lovett-Turner as the Mother

Abbess and Dave Simmons as Captain von Trapp. This was to be the Society's final performance as Salisbury Amateur Operatic Society. They rebranded the group Musical Theatre Salisbury, in keeping with their modern-day approach to theatre.

The staging of a production at the City Hall is no cheap affair. One hundred years ago, a show could be staged for £17. In 2012, this figure can be as high as £50,000 (you read that correctly!) The hire of the Hall can cost about £12,000 for a run of nights, the hire of the costumes can cost £3,000, the scenery can cost £3,000, a director will also cost about the same…and that is before the musical director, pianist, hire of rehearsal halls and other incidentals have been taken into account.

The Society has in many respects remained a family affair. Alison Babey, who very kindly helped with aspects of this book, followed in the footsteps of her parents who were involved in the group since the Fifties.

Joyce Bowden, Vice-President and a member for sixty-plus years, succinctly sums up the relationship between the City Hall and Musical Theatre Salisbury:

"The staff of the City Hall are (and have always) been a joy to work with and the stewards are always helpful – I can't fault them."

It is an amazing and creative group that now boasts between 60-70 members.

Please support it.

At the turn of the Century, Salisbury District Council made a significant investment in the auditorium by replacing the automated, tiered seating that had been installed back in 1985. Since then, there has also been significant investment back stage as well as to the technical facilities. The heavily used meeting rooms also received an upgrade.

Improvements were made to the Front of House and if you look up in the foyer area, you will see that some subtle but nevertheless thoughtful improvements have been made to the art-deco ceiling, not least the installation of some sympathetic lighting.

One of the themes which runs through this book is the fact that the City Hall is a war memorial – it was partially bought and converted with money donated by the citizens of Salisbury. However, whilst it was indeed a bona fide memorial, no one had thought to register it in the Schedule of War Memorials maintained by the Imperial War Museum. In or around 2009, a former Councillor (and a former member of the City Hall Sub-Committee), Colin Dullar, took it upon himself to add the Hall to the aforementioned Schedule.

It was also in 2009 that the Hall changed ownership. On the first day of April 2009, the Wiltshire (Structural Change) Order 2008 came into force. This dissolved Salisbury District Council (along with Kennet, North Wiltshire and West Wilshire Councils) replacing them with one unitary authority – Wiltshire Council. The new owners carried out some rebranding at the Hall and affirmed their dedication to maintain the City Hall as one of Wiltshire's premier entertainment centres.

It would have been impossible to cover every single event (approximately fifteen thousand bookings since 1963) but I hope this book gives you a flavour of what has been going on in the venue since Lady Radnor first declared it open on 18th September 1937; the staff that have worked tirelessly to keep it going, whether as a cinema or a centre for family entertainment and the individuals who have steered the Hall on and off the rocks again.

Special mention must go to the Hall's Sound Engineer. Phil Manning has played his part in maintaining a consistently high standard of work for over twenty years. Few people have had cause to complain about events being inaudible, two quiet or too loud. That is down to Phil's skill, hard work and professionalism.

I shall leave the final word to some of the current staff:

Samantha Peters, Marketing Manager:

"I love being a part of team that makes it possible for audiences to come and experience a show. When the show audience starts to come through our main doors, it's great to see people smiling with anticipation, and children are always really excited which is great."

Manager, Phill Smith:

"My vision for the City Hall is to leave a lasting legacy for the people of Salisbury who saved it from a fate worse than bingo and to those who have given their support ever since."

Councillor Mrs Scott, Phill Smith, staff and friends celebrate fifty years of the City Hall, 30th January 2013

(City Hall 2013)

NOVA PILBEAM FILMOGRAPHY

Little Friend (1934)
The Man Who Knew Too Much (1934)
Tudor Rose (1936)

Young And Innocent (1937)
Cheer Boys Cheer (1939)
Pastor Hall (1940)
Spring Meeting (1940)
Banana Ridge (1941)
The Next Of Kin (1942)
The Yellow Canary (1943)
Out Of Chaos (1944)
Men Of Science (1944)
Man Is Mine (1946)
Green Fingers (1947)
The Three Weird Sisters (1948)
Counter Blast (1948)

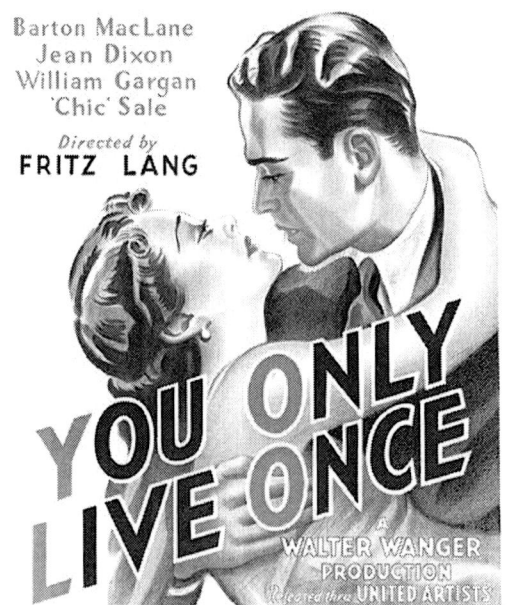

SALISBURY AMATEUR OPERATIC SOCIETY/MUSICAL THEATRE SALISBURY PRODUCTIONS AT THE CITY HALL

Calamity Jane (1990) (Peta Sebright)

Oklahoma (1963)
Trial By Jury (1964)

The Pirates of Penzance (1964)
Show Boat (1964
Vagabond King (1965)
Brigadoon (1965)
Carousel (1966)
The Gondoliers (1966)
The New Moon (1967)
Orpheus in the Underworld (1967)
The Mikado (1968)
The Pyjama Game (1968)
The Desert Song (1969)
The Count of Luxembourg (1969)
H.M.S Pinafore (1970)
Cox and Box (1970)
Kiss Me Kate (1970)
My Fair Lady (1971)
La Belle Helene (1971)
Princess Ida (1972)
Waltzes From Vienna (1972)
The Student Prince (1973)
Fiddler on the Roof (1973)
Ruddigore (1974)
Viva Mexico (1974)
The Merry Widow (1975)
The Yeoman of the Guard (1975)
Lilac Time (1976)
Half a Sixpence (1976)
Hello Dolly (1977)
Tom Jones (1977)
Trial by Jury &The Pirates of Penzance (1978)
Die Fledermaus (1978)
The Gondoliers (1979)
Bless the Bride (1979)
The Mikado (1980)
Annie Get Your Gun (1980)
Iolanthe (1981)
Kismet (1981)
H.M.S Pinafore (1982)
The Gypsy Baron (1982)

Patience (1983)
75th Anniversary Gala Performance (1983)
The Land of Smiles (1983)
Oklahoma! (1984)

Picture - The Gondoliers (1979)

Salisbury Festival Concert (1984)
Carmen (1984)
Fiddler on the Roof (1986)
South Pacific (1986)
The Pirates of Penzance (1987)
Guys and Dolls (1987)
Orpheus in the Underworld (1988)
The Sound Of Music (1988)
The Music Man (1989)
Annie (1989)
Calamity Jane (1990)
My Fair Lady (1990)

Carousel (1991)
Jesus Christ Superstar (1991)
Kiss Me Kate (1991)
The Yeoman of the Guard (1992)
Hans Anderson (1992)
Sweet Charity (1993)
Half a Sixpence (1993)
Showstoppers (1994)
Anything Goes (1994)
When the Lights Go On Again (1995)
Showboat (1995)
Showstoppers Encore! (1996)
Cabaret (1996)
The Mikado (1997)
Barnum (1997)
Me And My Girl (1998)
A Christmas Old Time Musical (1998)
Rhythms of Life (1999)
South Pacific (1999)
The Pirates of Penzance (2000)
Oliver! (2000)
Guys And Dolls (2001)
The Wizard of Oz (2001)
The Merry Widow (2002)
Fiddler on the Roof (2002)
Orpheus in the Underworld (2003)
Oklahoma! (2003)
H.M.S Pinafore (2004)
Annie (2004)
Songs of the Silver Screen (2005)
Scrooge (2005)
Hello Dolly! (2006)
My Fair Lady (2006)
Iolanthe (2007)
Titanic the Musical (2007)
The Pirates of Penzance (2008)
The King and I (2008)
The Mikado (2009)
The Full Monty (2010)

42nd Street (2010)
The Gondoliers (2011)
The Sound of Music (2011)
The Wizard of Oz (2012)

Carmen (1984) (John Pinder)

ACKNOWLEDGEMENTS, CREDITS AND THANKS

With my sincere thanks (in no particular order):

The Salisbury Journal, Barbara Softley, Roger Elliott, Henry Wills, Graham Jackson, Bryan Rowe, Colette McCarraher, Phill Smith, Phil Manning, Victoria Bell, Sam Peters, Malcolm McCarraher, Frogg Moody, Richard Nash, Ken & Beryl Robson, Muriel Eldridge, Betty Noack, Iain Barnes, Christine Gilbert, Roger Collins, Joyce Bowden, Mike Reeve (we miss you), Sam at www.ledzeppelin.com, www.beatlesbible.com, Peter Coombs, Mike Doherty, Ian Hussey, Hazel Strand, Roger Godwin, Colin Dullar, Anglo Italian and Hack at Wrestling Heritage, Steve Mitchell (for wrestling memorabilia), Ray Plunkett wrestling referee (for wrestling memorabilia), Tony Scalo, Mike and Sandy Weeks, Ken Harris, Dee Adcock (SAOS reviews), Kevin Catchpole (SAOS reviews), Alec J Ruddick (SAOS reviews), Doug Goodman ('Mr Pastry'), 'Big' Jim Everett (we miss you), Allison Babey (SAOS), the Futcher family, all the staff of Salisbury City Hall, past and present.

Bibliography:

David Bowie - Any Day Now by Kevin Cann (Adelita Limited).
Hellraiser by Ginger Baker (John Blake)
Hold Tight – Voices of the Sarum Sound 1945-1969 by Frogg Moody & Richard Nash.
Endless Beat – Voices of the New Sarum Sound – 1970-1999 by Frogg Moody & Richard Nash.
www.wrestlingheritage.co.uk
www.salisburyamateuroperatic.org.uk/

PHOTOGRAPHS

Phill Smith with Jimmy Carr poster – Richard Coombs
The Toast is 60 Years of the City Hall – from Salisbury Journal.
The Story of the City Hall - Part One Cover photograph – Daily Sketch
The Original Picture House – courtesy of Alan Richardson
Vestibule 1937 – Futcher and Son
Inner Vestibule 1937 – Futcher and Son
Sketch of Auditorium – Gaumont British
Staff group photograph 1937 – Futcher and Son
Opening Day - cover of the Daily Sketch
Opening Day Audience – Daily Sketch
George Howes – Gaumont British
Nova Pilbeam and Betty Street – Daily Sketch
Noval Pilbeam and Lady Radnor – Daily Sketch
Nova Pilbeam portrait – Gaumont British
The Programme – Gaumont British with thanks to Alan Richardson
Betty Bush - Betty Noack
Len on Roof of New Picture House – courtesy of Christine Gilbert
Len and Ken at the Window - courtesy of Christine Gilbert
Focke-Wulf – unknown
Stage Presentation – courtesy of Ken and Beryl Robson
'Frieda' – Futcher and Son
'The Big Heart' – Futcher and Son
Projection Room (front) – Futcher and Son
Projection Room (back) – Futcher and Son
Two Projectors – Futcher and Son
Len Loading Projector – Futcher and Son
Odeon frontage – courtesy of Christine Gilbert
Elephant Foot Projector (single) – Futcher and Son
Elephant Foot Projectors (pair) – Futcher and Son
Len at the Twin Turntables – Futcher and Son
'Richard III' – courtesy of Christine Gilbert
Parachute Frontage – courtesy of Christine Gilbert

'The White Unicorn' - courtesy of Christine Gilbert
'The Chiltern Hundreds' - courtesy of Christine Gilbert
'The Browning Version' – courtesy of Christine Gilbert
City Hall 1963 - Salisbury Journal
The Original Salisbury Playhouse – unknown
All wrestling posters and flyers - courtesy of Ray Plunkett
Wrestlers photos courtesy of Anglo Italian and Hack at Wrestling Heritage
BEN Ball – Wendy Houston
Beatles autographs - courtesy of Christine Gilbert
Phill Smith by DDDBM&T plaque – Richard Coombs
DDDBM&T - Salisbury Journal
DDDBM&T - Salisbury Journal
Mike Weeks – James McCarraher
City Hall 'Oklahoma' frontage – courtesy of Musical Theatre Salisbury
Viva Mexico Programme - courtesy of Musical Theatre Salisbury
Die Fledermaus - courtesy of Musical Theatre Salisbury (photographer: Peter Brown)
Guys and Dolls - courtesy of Musical Theatre Salisbury (photographer: Peter Brown)
The Gypsy Baron - courtesy of Musical Theatre Salisbury (photographer: Peter Brown)
Iolanthe - courtesy of Musical Theatre Salisbury (photographer: Peter Brown)
Hello Dolly - courtesy of Musical Theatre Salisbury (photographer: Peter Brown)
Land of Smiles - courtesy of Musical Theatre Salisbury (photographer: Peter Brown)
South Pacific - courtesy of Musical Theatre Salisbury (photographer: Ken Babey)
Cabinet Opening - courtesy of Musical Theatre Salisbury
Camel in Foyer – courtesy of Alan Richardson
City Hall (Eighties) – Salisbury Journal
Front entrance derelict – courtesy of the City Hall
All internal renovation photographs - courtesy of the City Hall
Fairport Convention – Salisbury Journal (photographer: Roger Elliott)
South Wilts Grammar Prom - Salisbury Journal

David Rawlinson - Salisbury Journal
Barbara Softley - Salisbury Journal
Rik Mayall - Salisbury Journal
Toyah - Salisbury Journal (photographer: Roger Elliott)
'The Doctor' - Salisbury Journal (photographer: Roger Elliott)
Lee Brilleaux - Salisbury Journal (photographer: Roger Elliott)
The Dubliners - Salisbury Journal (photographer: Roger Elliott)
Wrestling (wrestlers un-named) – Mike Weeks
'My Hall's a Stick of Rock' - Salisbury Journal
Peter Green - Salisbury Journal (photographer: Roger Elliott)
Supergrass – Chris Carter
Fifty years of the City Hall - Salisbury Journal (photographer: Roger Elliott)
Auditorium 2013 front – Richard Coombs
Auditorium 2013 back – Richard Coombs
The Girl Was Young poster – Gaumont British
You Only Live Once poster - Gaumont British
Calamity Jane - courtesy of Musical Theatre Salisbury (photographer: Peter Brown)
The Gondoliers - courtesy of Musical Theatre Salisbury (photographer: Peter Brown)
Carmen - courtesy of Musical Theatre Salisbury (photographer: Peter Brown)

Lightning Source UK Ltd.
Milton Keynes UK
UKOW02f1323200516

274648UK00001B/194/P